M000230055

DESTINATION COMMUNITY

DAVID TWIGGS

DESTINATION COMMUNITY

THE EVOLUTION OF TRAVEL, TOURISM, LEISURE, AND COMMUNITY

—

With Social Commentary by
Dr. Yang Luo-Branch Ph.D

A DISTINCT PRESS BOOK

DISTINCT PRESS PUBLISHING

Book Cover Design: Susan Veach
Cover Photograph: Eric Dugan Photography

If you are interested in professional review copies of this book because you intend to write a review in your publication, mention this book on your radio show or podcast, post about it to your blog or website, or if you request an article or interview, you may contact the author directly at (864) 378-2139.

For more information visit: www.DavidTwiggs.com

Summary: Building and enhancing a community into a tourism destination is often one of the most misunderstood and under utilized economic development tools available today. This book explains the steps to take to build a strong tourism destination while keeping your community a great place to live. Strengthen tourism as an economic driver without losing what you love about your community.

1. Social Sciences : Urban Planning & Development 2. Architecture : Urban & Land Use Planning 3. Politics & Social Sciences : Social Sciences : Human Geography

Library of Congress Cataloging-in-Publication Data
2015939553

Twiggs, David 1964 -
Destination Community: The Evolution of Travel, Tourism,
Leisure, and Community

ISBN-10:1943103038
ISBN-13:978-1-943103-03-4

Printed in the United States of America
10 9 8 7 6 5 4 3 2 1

CONTENTS

ACKNOWLEDGEMENTS I
—

I would like to thank my wife Ashley and my daughters, Salem and CeCe, for being at my side through many projects as I collected the experience necessary to bring many years of strategies, plans and gambles to culmination. Thanks for always encouraging me to stay on the edge and keep my flow on.

I would like to thank my parents for instilling in me that there is no easy road to being the best at something.

I want to thank Dr. Yang Luo Branch for seeing and explaining the academic value to my theories that I had been so unscientifically testing on the real world for the last 20 years. Your explanations add to the understanding even though my organic streaming and your academic rigor didn't always align easily.

I want to specifically thank Kirk Smith who worked with me daily putting together the Little River Blueway, a comprehensive effort specifically pulling together my smaller project concepts at other projects into a conscious integrated tourism system. The planning document attached in the appendix was largely due to Kirk's masterful ability to distill my abstract concepts into an understandable document while adding his own spin. You added much value and I know you will continue to grow the economic and livability potential of the Little River Blueway Region of South Carolina. As my Director of Marketing for 8 years, Kirk understood that marketing couldn't make up for a product problem and constantly pushed for me to develop new lifestyle products.

To all my sporting cohorts who continue to be part of my past and future projects, Matt Fussell of the Homestead Resort, Brownie Liles of the Watauga River Lodge, and John Higgins of CSM Shooting. Thanks for your help and friendship over the years.

David

ACKNOWLEDGEMENTS II
—

First of all, I would like to express my gratitude to David. I appreciate the opportunity to work with an experienced and dedicated community maker and thinker as he is. At one point, I was concerned about the completely different cultural background as well as non-overlapped training and professional paths that David and I have. Then I realized that we, together with our colleagues and peers in the profession, share the same passion to make better places for people to visit, live and enjoy life. The very differences between David and I actually make the book unique. Upon finishing the book, not only have I learned a great deal from reading David's manuscript, but it was also a good practice for me to relearn, rethink and re-express what I thought was the knowledge I already had.

I also owe this to Dr. Yungmei Tsai, an Emeritus Professor in Sociology at Texas Tech University. In Dr. Tsai's highly achieving some 40 years of teaching and research career in Urban Sociology, I consider myself very fortunate to be his last student before his retirement. He oversaw me as my academic advisor finishing my master's and doctoral programs at Texas Tech University, taught me to view and appreciate people and places from sociological perspective, which you will see a lot in this book. To me, he is one of those people who I met and changed my life.

I want to express my upmost gratitude to my family. My husband, Andrew Branch, showed me the best love and friendship:

he listens when I needed someone to bounce off thoughts, and gives me support and encouragement unconditionally, always. My parents, who are in China that I have not seen in almost two years and miss every day, are my motivation to work hard and grow.

Last but not least, I am thankful to my colleagues at Hot Springs Village and my teammates at Village Placemaking. I am also thankful to the help of Ashley Twiggs in editing this book and her effort in making it better.

Dr. Yang Luo-Branch

OVERVIEW AND THE OBJECTIVES OF THIS BOOK

—

This book intends to layout the components of creating an Integrated Tourism System for Destination Communities. These concepts can be used to develop destination communities in urban as well as rural settings. To build an understanding of this process the following areas will be discussed:

- Opportunities Resulting From Value and Behavioral Shifts In Specific Target Markets
- Using Complimentary Subcultures as Basis for Building Specific Destinations
- Understanding Subcultures and Human Capital
- Integrated System Model
- Cataloging System Assets and Creating Narrative of Place
- Growth and Maturation of Destination Communities

In addition, Appendix I is a full planning report from the Planning Stages of the Little River Blueway Project. This will give some examples of the early thinking as we developed what has come to be known as an Integrated Tourism System. Special thanks to Kirk Smith who compiled the LRB report with me. Kirk succeeded me as Chief Operating Officer of Savannah Lakes Village and is carrying on that work.

LIST OF KEY CONCEPTS
—

There are a few basic definitions that are helpful to be familiar with at the onset:

1. **Subculture and Culture** – Subculture is the "tribe" or wholehearted user group for any specific activity. For example: Outdoor Recreation is a Culture. Paddlers, Mountain Bikers, Skiers, Trail Runners, Equestrians, Golfers, or Climbers are examples of Subcultures. The Arts is a Culture. Musicians, Sculptors, Painters, Crafters, Wood Workers, Glass Blowers and Writers are subcultures. Subcultures may or may not be compatible for sharing the same resources. These resources may be the natural physicality of a region or the type of hospitality, provision and entertainment preferences of a particular subculture. Some subcultures are difficult to mix on the same resources. Some tolerate each other given proper separation and scheduling while others thrive from the relationship.

2. **Complimentary Subcultures** – Subcultures that share similar values, often sharing the same physicality, region or space at the same time, through scheduling or in different seasons. These often share similar appreciation for the natural and cultural resources of a region.

3. **Conservation Community** – Community design based on preserving the best assets (natural or cultural) for the general use of the community. This spreads the value gravity of an asset throughout the community rather than concentrate it only on a few premium real estate locations.

4. **Corporate Monoculture Tourism System** – A single or affiliated corporate structure being the single cultural and economic driver within a region. In tourism, the Disney Corporation is a prime example of a destination being developed based on a corporate monoculture.

5. **Formula Community** – A community model based on a replicable and predictable financial model that proliferated during the 40 years prior to the 2008 real estate collapse. These are generically called the "golf and gates" model. Some of these were well designed based on an organic quality of place and allowed the natural evolution of community. Many more were simply replicated as urban sprawl with little, if any, natural quality of place. The communities based on poor fundamentals have experienced struggles remaining relevant in the current marketplace.

6. **Destination Community** – A destination community is a community that reaps significant economic benefits from tourism while remaining livable and engaging to the full and part time residents. The tourism draw typically comes from relating complimentary subcultures based on the natural and cultural resources authentic to the area. It aims to provide its people, both long-term residents, seasonal and the visitors, a sense of belonging and authentic connection with people and quality of life. These communities are established based on a set of complementary sub-cultures and feature careful planning and design to meet the higher levels of human needs according to Maslow's five hierarchies of human needs.

7. **Handcrafted Tourism** – This is my term for carefully crafting a mixture of subcultures that will engage in both the use and protection of the resources of the area creating a destination community. This creates room for local/visitor relationships and a sense of belonging that differs from tourism based on a simple entertainment model.

8. **In-migration** – The population of people moving into an area. Often a significant revenue source through increasing tax base from housing growth and sales, business opportunities for support services, and importing a significant disposable income to spend in your region.

9. **Slow Culture** – The culture of an area when it has been allowed to naturally evolve over time. A separation from or misunderstanding of an area's slow culture is often a key mistake in new development; which found it easier to use a formula model rather than a customized authentic model true to the area's slow culture.

10. **Tourism Destination** – The area or region has a tourism system as a significant part of the local economy where people choose to go to spend discretionary time and money. The area must have the ability to meet the recreational, provision, hospitality, and lodging needs of the visitor. This can be based on a corporate monoculture such as the Disney products or a collection of complimentary subcultures such as Charleston, SC or Blowing Rock, NC.

11. **Integrated Tourism System** – A destination organized in such a way that the visitor experience is understandable to the potential visitors prior to the trip. This is based on an understanding of the needs and preferences of particular subcultures that are naturally attracted to the asset base of the region. This base culture allows other complimentary subculture to be targeted and served to increase the tourism usage of the area. Simultaneously, controls are built to determine the potential downside to further development as a destination community. It is the integration of the authentic potential of the area, the complimentary subcultures that will be engaged by that potential, the combination of appropriate services and the long-term controls to conserve and enhance both the tourism assets and livability of the community.

12. **Value Shift** – A significant change in American cultural values are moving away from false expectations of fulfillment based on conspicuous consumerism, hedonic and luxury since the 1950's; to a lifestyle of appreciating genuine interaction with people, authentic experience in nature, and introspective connection with self in the recent years. While by no means an across the board cultural shift, it is significant enough in the tourism sector to generate new opportunities and reduce the relevance of some established destination community models.

13. **Place** – Place is extremely important to me because it is the culmination of the collective natural assets, history, culture and current interface with the people. Sense of Place and Quality of Place are terms used to further express the holistic nature of the term.

Preface

IT IS ABOUT CONSCIOUS TOURISM

This is a business book. Much more than that, this is a book that teaches us a kind of attitude and a way of thinking. It is about being conscious about what we do and how we experience. Tourism? Ok, let's talk about tourism.

I have a broad definition for tourism, which is the adventure to experience something new, spectacular and impressive with wonder and awe, and feel the joy of learning from such experience. In this sense, we all start out being a tourist, whether we were aware of it or not. In those early years after we were born, we open our eyes each day, spending our awaking moment looking around. We were filled with curiosity and the passion for trying something new. We were a little scared, a little hesitant, and we didn't know what to expect. Slowly, we began to pick up skills to navigate through this journey that we call life: we learned how to move around with our legs, instead of our hands; we learned how to speak a language and start to make sense, instead of making noises and crying. We met new people, remembered the names of new things, as we continue to look around in this new world. By the time our parents let us out of the house with friends – the outside world suddenly became a wonderland, and our adventure has not stopped.

Fast-forward many years; we have travelled, moved, and maybe moved back to where we started. Our adventure is stretched, and our knowledge and skills have accumulated. However, somewhere in the journey, we forgot to wonder, to be awed or be impressed. We go through daily life as a routine, living by reaction. We still look, but not really see; we hear everything, without truly listening. We think we know all the answers to this adventure, and no longer seek to learn: learning about this world as well as ourselves. It takes more and more for us to get excited. So we go on expensive exotic trips or pay high prices to get ourselves high, just to pursue that original glance of feeling wondered, awed and excited like we experienced when we were younger. We choose to escape, rather than trying to find a sense of belonging in what we have and who we are.

—

Destination community is different from a traditional tourist destination. A traditional tourist spot or destination is intended for people to come to visit and leave. People will stay for a brief experience, and they have every right to expect the trip to offer some pop that will give them an instant satisfaction. They may come back, or they may not. Although the latter is much likely, even when people do come back, the tourist spot is not a place for them to stay and never leave again, where they enjoy being a guest, and the tourist spot simply serves the guest. But the two never intend to belong to each other.

A destination community is also different from a traditional community, or we may call a neighborhood, where we go and buy a house, expecting it to be safe for long term living. We care about the floor plan of our house, we care about how big our yard is, and how far is it from our house to the closest grocery store. Our expectation for the community is clear and simple: we just want to find a place where we can come home to at the end of the day. When we want to take a break from our daily routine, we pack and leave to take a tourist trip somewhere else.

Most people have experience with both kinds of the community: we have to choose between adventure and home. Destination communities break this kind of stereotype thinking for you: you visit a place, if you like, you stay longer, or you never have to leave.

A beautiful ancient tale from over 1500 years ago, *Peach Blossom Spring*, written by one of the most famous Chinese poets Tao Yuanming (365-427 A.D.) from Jin Dynasty, told us a beautiful story. There was a fisherman walking up a creek to find a good spot to fish. He left his boat and hiked miles and miles in the mountain and got lost. Suddenly, he entered an area of peach trees with beautiful blossoms. He was stunned by the beauty of the scene and decided walk deeper into it (see Figure 1.) As the creek led him to the end of the peach tree wooded area, he reached the origin of the creek and saw a spring coming out from the earth and a hill in front of him. Curious about the light coming from a grotto on the hill, he went forward to see what was on the other side of the opening. After he squeezed himself through the tunnel for about ten steps, he was presented a bright, wide-open and harmonious village scene:

> The land is flat, and houses are neat. There are good farm fields, beautiful ponds, and mulberry trees are orderly arrayed next to thick bamboo groves. The streets and alleys are connected, where he could hear chickens and dogs walking on them. The villagers are busying themselves with farming activities. Men and women dressed just like people from the outside. The elderly and children are taking good care of each other and enjoying the relaxing time.

The whole village, although surprised to see the fisherman, treated him very friendly. Villagers gathered to see him and asked where he was from, and served him with the best food and drinks. He felt very much welcomed and was very happy. He stayed for a few days, and finally said goodbye to the village (see Figure 2). He went back out through the grotto, and returned through the same route and found his boat where he left it. When he was trying to go back with several people a few days later, he was never able to find this village again at the Peach Blossom Spring.

Figure 1: A painting depicts the Peach Blossom Spring plot (painting by a famous Chinese modern artist, Feng Zikai.)

Figure 2: A painting depicts the Peach Blossom Spring (ancient painting, painter unknown, from the collection in Summer Palace, Beijing, China)

Destination Community is intended to be a place like Peach Blossom Spring, where people are attracted to visit, enjoy the stay and decide to return and stay longer, because they feel welcomed and belong. To achieve this, we, who work in the profession of building destination communities, are dedicated in building the community base on local resources and cultural atmosphere, in creating thoughtfully designed and detailed environment, and in catering to the needs and hobbies of the residents and visitors. We call it "handmade," because we want to give you a comforting and heartfelt experience similar to when you put on a pair of handmade leather shoes from Italy. The luxury is not in the price tag, but in the unique and rare experience.

The only difference from the *Peach Blossom Spring* story is that our story will have a good ending. We want you to be able to find the authentic experience of our destination community again, come back and make it home if you'd like.

—

This book calls for the attention for both sides of the fence: people that are taking an adventure (as a tourist or just in life generally) and those who are creating adventures (again, for tourism community or for oneself in life). Granted, from a professional point of view, it is the community makers' job to build the physical infrastructure of an environment. But for a culture or experience to grow, it requires us to first be an open-minded human to be able to appreciate living life, and to discover the potentials in a place and people (including ourselves), no matter which side of the fence you are. Indeed, it is one of our hopes through the book to wake up our own consciousness about what we do and how we experience.

Handmade tourism is about letting the tourists and tourism destination to meet in the middle. For a destination community to work, tourists need to start to live life more wholeheartedly, continue to learn and relearn on the adventures and get to know themselves. For the community to become a destination community, community makers need to create more detailed and subtle attraction of interest, to develop fully based on local resources to stay authentic, and to foster subcultures to meet every need of the visitors. We want that connection, where people, including ourselves, enjoy the trip, want to come again, stay longer and in-migrate to make it home.

—

David has over 20 years of community building, management and leadership experience. He has keen observations, insights, thoughts and visions for building better contemporary communities. He has been documenting all these by writing throughout the years. David provides his insights from his entrepreneurial, business, and placemaking philosophy point of view. This is the meat of the book. *Building Destination Community*, which is David's original "recipe" for improving the community models that are no longer working well in the current American society. My main contribution is adding illustration and diagrams that hopefully will help our readers to understand the concepts and message we are trying to communicate. I also highlight some of his key points throughout the book, and explain why these have proven true from a sociological point of view. David and I share a common general understanding like this (see Figure 3):

Figure 3: Sociology and business point of view both help us learn how to build a good community.

Although the diagram above is over simplified by not including many other important factors in working on building a good community, David and I believe it is important to view our profession in a big picture. Introducing business and sociology points of view could be helpful for us to get a broader understanding. Also by including these two areas, we believe there are some universal reasons for what is a good community for across the human race, regardless of culture, continents and the language we speak. That being said, we invite, welcome and appreciate people that are willing to add elements to this bubble diagram – what we are doing through this book is to simply open a conversation.

This book begins with where does the concept of "destination community" come from, how does it work and where to go from here – how it develops and matures. We see the shifts in cultural values in the American society since the 1950's, which results from the economic prosperity and technology advancement. The culture shift brings forward the changes in people's lifestyle, when people became more and more distant from the agrarian based living. Later, the shift in community models and tourism experience is discussed. As the formula community, as David calls it, rises and declines, the concept of Destination Community, as a more sustainable tourism based community, is introduced. The new generation of in-migration is becoming smarter in choosing their community. We explore the main characteristics of a destination community, why David calls it "handmade" experience, and why people are attracted by it. It all comes down to connecting authentic and versatile "subcultures" fostered by a supportive business environment. Later we look at theory and examples to explain a supportive business environment, namely "Integrated Tourism System", and how to design such a system. In David's opinion, this is a key to the success of a destination community. We lay out the vision of the future growth beyond the initial phases of building a destination community, where all readers are invited to imagine with us, work with us and proceed with hope, creativity, passion, and thoughtfulness.

As it is already said, this book is intended for all of you, and all of us – we all live, in a community; we all travel, travel to places and travel in life. If you accept my definition of "tourism" that I shared with you at the beginning, then we have all been tourists – and will probably still choose to embark on tourist trips, by my definition or in a strict tourism sense. No matter, where you choose to go and where to stay, we want you to have a great experience. Please accept this book as an invitation to become more mindful, conscious, and curious with us as we move forward. Enjoy your adventure!

Dr. Yang Luo Branch

finished in the Library of Bowen Law School
at University of Arkansas in Little Rock

Chapter 1

VALUE SHIFTS TOWARDS TOURISM AND RELOCATION DESTINATIONS

We are now faced with creating and recreating destination communities to meet a new set of values that have rapidly shifted from the prerecession model. Perhaps it was the financial reality check that accelerated the already growing shift in values into the mainstream. Many have shifted from seeking a tourist experience to wanting to feel a sense of belonging and experience self-discovery, when we travel, invest in a second home or look for a quality place for retirement. After all, who wants to be treated as a tourist?

America's Value Shift In Culture Since The 1950's

When we speak of a value shift, it begs the question: from what? Dr. Brene Brown, *Daring Greatly* author and research professor at the University of Houston, explains that to start living wholeheartedly, we need to move away from a culture where being preoccupied, over scheduled and over connected has become a status symbol. We have become well familiar with technology, industrialization and automation of tasks that formally were part of basic home economics. It has not only created a lifestyle free of what many consider preindustrial "drudgery",

1

but it has also disconnected us from the basic human processes of thousands of years.

I feel there was a major mind shift in the 1950's. It could first be seen in basic home economics. This time period held the rapid expansion of processed industrial food distribution. Prior to this, virtually all food was whole food and slow food. While not necessarily organic, it had simpler inputs and no genetic modification. Most meals required cooking, which meant planning, and most homes had at least a kitchen garden in the backyard (see Figure 4) and laid food by for winter. The majority of the United States population was living in a rural setting. The 1950's marked a clear turning point: from the valuing of the agrarian home economics and self-reliant thinking into a consumer based lifestyle ideal. The prosperous Americans bought the wonderful new prepackaged foods in the new supermarkets. It was a new ideal being set for the American Dream. Gardening and putting food by was now considered only for the poor.

Figure 4: Home economics cooking class ("Home economics in public schools. Kitchen in housekeeping flat, New York," circa 1910. National Photo Company Collection glass negative.).

Natural urban growth fell quickly to an auto centric planning mentality. The growth of air conditioning allowed America to move inside and the importance of the porch diminished, as it was no longer the most comfortable place to be during the heat of the day. From the 1950's through the 1980's, the mainstream American dream became substantially based on an auto driven, processed food, air conditioned consumerism. Within a single generation we went from totally analog to digital culture, from segregated to diversity, from the local paper to the Internet, and from agrarianism to urbanism.

All these "conveniences" created a great insulator. As a nation, we were rapidly losing knowledge of the fundamentals that were basic to the generations before us. It insulated us from the rhythms of nature. We no longer needed to produce nor prepare our food (see Figure 5). The booming of automobiles and supermarkets insulated us from a requirement to live a life of face-to-face connectivity. As Rowan Williams, the former Archbishop of Canterbury described it in an interview with Krista Tippet for *On Being*, we are losing the "craft of being a creature."

Figure 5: *Food shopping in supermarket (Village Ad of Dupont Cellophane, 1952)*

Kurt Andersen began the conversation about a great reset in American values in his 2009 book, *Reset: How this Crises can Restore our Values and Renew America.* He and others speak of a "new frugality" that has resulted from values being shifted away from a consumption-based mentality. Conspicuous con-

sumption has lost favor as a value proposition and is being re-
placed with a value for simpler and more honest and authentic
experience. This includes a shift away from credit-based lifestyle. Less use of debt by Americans doesn't always show as
positive in our traditional macro economic metrics but a new
vitality can be created in formally marginalized places being
rediscovered and appreciated as destinations. The benefit of the
local shops, restaurants, cafes and services being supported by a
shift to simpler destination livability can be significant.

Value Shift For Destination Community

It is important to remember that there are multiple facets to
tourism economic development. Economic growth comes from
visitation: heads in beds, feet on fairways, etc. Another side of
this comes from in-migration. People want to retire or buy second homes in the areas that they love to visit. An issue with
early style destination community models is that they focused
on developing in-migration housing in the generally desirable
regions, but overlaid it with generic amenity and lifestyle options that could be found in many similar destination communities throughout the country; regardless of the nature of the place
these were being developed.

Beginning in the 1950's, it wasn't simply that modern conveniences made America feel that traditional knowledge and skills
were irrelevant. Popular culture created an urban and suburban
contempt for the agrarian lifestyle. Proliferation of television
created new images of the ideal lifestyle as one of ease, convenience and sophistication. The popular media portrayed the hay-
seed farmer, the bumpkin and other stereotypes showing igno-
rance of the rural class even though most Americans had much
of their immediate family remaining in rural or semi-agrarian
lifestyles. This was reinforced with a television viewpoint of
the good life consisting of Ward and June Cleaver heading off
to the country club, Tony Nelson taking Jeannie to the officers

club, or Thurston Howell the III getting Gilligan to help build the island golf club. While these were designed for comic relief, they all permeated the illusion of the Norman Rockwell perfect traditional family setting down for Thanksgiving dinner or the Madison Avenue sophistication as the norm. These juxtaposed stereotypes created both an inferiority complex and dissatisfaction with agrarian lifestyle and a false sense of what would be a satisfying lifestyle.

Developers used this mindset shift on what the average American was told created the "good life" to create early generation lifestyle destinations. They were simply responding to the general desires of the market as it had been conditioned. Many of these destination developers actually did forward-thinking community planning, considering the general lack of sophistication in the planning world at the time. These early communities were completely new creatures and that made them unique and attractive in themselves (see Figure 6). This quickly evolved into the "Gates and Golf" formula model. This same basic community type proliferated throughout the US because the capital market and bankers understood the model. During the last housing boom, the model accelerated with even less creativity, imagination, and quality of place. Basically if you created housing with gates and golf you were unique enough.

Figure 6: A corporate monoculture in Las Vegas ("Fremont Street 1952 at night" by Edward N. Edstrom, 1952).

5

After forty plus years of development this model is no longer unique. Status quo is unacceptable. *The value of experiences is overtaking the value of exclusivity.* Communities based on inauthentic lifestyle expectations are now experiencing a loss of relevance in the face of changing values. With the current value evolution or reset, a large segment of the baby boomer and following generations are changing their value judgment to balance modern techno bombardment with an organic connection to the natural world (see Figure 7). The value of access is surpassing the need for ownership. Commonality and diversity are overtaking insular isolationism. Paths are replacing fences. Gates are welcoming concierge stations rather than roadblocks to "check your papers." Gardens are valued as much as golf courses. The authentic local has become the exotic. The attraction for commoditized monoculture is being rapidly lost to the value of the unique, the individual, the handmade and extraordinary. Some destination developers began to feel this in the early 2000 and a few pioneers began talking about a new value proposition.

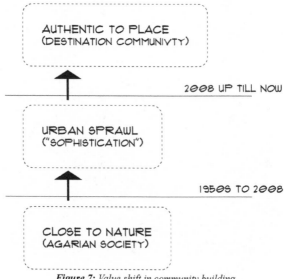

Figure 7: Value shift in community building

I feel that the most encouraging changes come from the value shift from consumerism to stewardship as a key personal value. "Stewardship is simply the caretaking of gifts" said Wendell Berry. We must build our destination models on the stewardship of unique resources in order to build extraordinary places. As the values shift, the loss of perceived value in the consumption of consumer products or the depletion of natural resources for our convenience has not changed universally. It has changed dramatically for the markets we are attracting and our development practices will have to be adjusted accordingly. You are not trying to attract everyone.

In the past, many experiences were designed to allow us to escape into artificial environments, and cultural evolution from the 1950's created a false sense of what builds a fulfilling lifestyle. Destination communities should seek to bring us into a different rhythm, show as another lifestyle point of view or seek to connect us to nature and the basic systems of being human. The common denominator in this value shift to more authentic experiences is a desire for greater understanding, physical and spiritual growth and renewal. For some this may be a place for adventure, meditation, or learning. Don't get the idea that these folks don't want high-end amenities, lodging and hospitality. A farm to table meal at one of chef/restaurateur Hugh Acheson's restaurants such as The Five and Ten in Athens, GA is not a low priced proposition. My point is the desires of folks with changing values create a new economic development opportunity that will not be served with a generic product.

From Zoned and Formula Community To Authentic Destination Community

In most of America, building the traditional mixed use downtown that we see in our best cities is now illegal due to our zoning ordinances. Many communities suffer from the results of years of poor planning practices. While there are very re-

7

markable communities that are notable exceptions, with the proliferation of the cookie cutter mass-produced housing units and the generic strip center, we have seen a homogenization of communities across America (see Figure 8). Traditional Euclidian Zoning practices have effectively segregated all the land use options. Subdivisions have segregated us by income. Under the normal mid 1980's Euclidian zoning model, land uses were separated. In new development, premium lake, golf and amenity front lots were given the sales focus with the remainder of the property given little consideration as to livability and sold at a discount. Historian Kenneth Jackson as early as 1985 in his book, *Crabgrass Frontier: The Suburbanization of the United States*, described that "Suburbia...is a manifestation of such fundamental characteristics of American society as conspicuous consumption, reliance upon the private automobile, upward mobility, the separation of the family nuclear units, the widening division between work and leisure, and the tendency toward racial and economic exclusiveness."

Figure 8: *Tract housing in Colorado Springs, Colorado. ("Suburbia by David Shankbone" by David Shankbone, 2008)*

In a 2012 discussion of Quality of Life and Experience within destination communities, Lauren Ponder, of the SC National Heritage Corridor, brought up the point that "People living in a community don't necessarily know or think they need anything." She understood that a community needs to supply opportunities for self-actualization beyond Maslow's lower level needs. I believe this is true on many levels.

Many residents of our communities live with a low-grade lack of fulfillment and general unease that is barely conscious to them. The 25 years preceding the real estate market meltdown in 2008, the planning for communities was rather course, unimaginative and uninspired. *Many moving into a community were sold a marketers vision of what the good life should be and if you don't enjoy this version of lifestyle, there is something wrong with you.* Because this lifestyle, which can often be inherently unfulfilling, is accepted as the "norm," people are fearful of exploring other options for fear of being out of the norm. If you look at Richard Florida's, *Rise of the Creative Class And How It's Transforming Work, Leisure, Community And Everyday Life,* community tolerance for and celebration of individuality, is a key economic driver in the creative class economy. I think the recent economic challenges have reshuffled the national value system allowing some space for this type of conversation and acceptance of other types of community and definitions of normal.

What is exciting about the post-recession tourism community industry is that there is no longer a tried and true formula for creating these destinations. You cannot succeed by being generic or average anymore. Even if a tourism community could, I would not want to waste my energy to simply churn out another cookie cutter destination. That eventually dilutes the livability and core culture of the region. I strive to build culture-based destinations that are fanatical about their unique values, passions and culture. That's where the fun is. Fun? Yes, but also serious business.

I was working in one of the most rural counties in the South that did not protect the integrity of their open space. In efforts to create an economic development project, thousands of acres of land were traditionally subdivided into the standards of one acre or less lots. While the plan had an excellent sales model and sold thousands of lots, infrastructure was snaked through the area with no connectivity or economy. Widespread overproduction of undiversified lots while eliminating the maintained open lands tying the areas together resulted in unbuilt but platted sprawl inflicted upon the landscape. Only about twenty percent of the originally planned units were built. The land was no longer maintained because the open farms and forestlands were reduced to insignificant small lots. A thousand acres could be farmed, grazed, or managed for timber; a thousand lots, one acre or less each could not. Even though the area is surrounded by plenty of public open lands, the poor planning within the "urbanized" area left the county, with an extremely low Return on Investment (ROI) on money spent maintaining miles of infrastructure.

While lamented for many years, the lack of new home construction in this destination community is now a godsend to the region. The real estate downturn experienced from 2008 to present has allowed the area to be reconfigured as investors have lost their stranglehold on the destination community. We brought logical assemblages of properties together to create areas for civic, commercial and residential space. It has allowed housing diversification and density transects radiating out from a ten-acre assemblage for mixed use village center location. While national housing trends still remain slow to grow; we are seeing more inquires than we have in the past eight years. The lack of initial building has not left us inundated with a housing stock of outdated and nondescript housing. We have put together large areas for smaller building units at prices that are both profitable to builders and attractive to the changing psychographics of the market. Obtained lakefront lots for conversion to micro parks to add value to interior lots by giving them lake access. Thereby, we were able to start building a destination community: this is how we can protect farms, our hometowns, and the woods and rivers of our youth.

Define The Core Values For Each Destination Community

Since generic is no longer acceptable, when you build your destination, you now must base it on a set of values and specific culture. Staying authentic and sincere to those values is vital. At a meeting a couple of years ago I was fortunate to listen to Bert Jacobs, the founder of "Life is Good," tell the story of he and his brother living out their van on the road while starting up their T-shirt business. Their Research and Design (R&D) was drawing pictures on the wall of their apartment and having friends pick a favorite to be their next design.

When the brand became so popular they were looking to get financing for expansion, the bankers said they had to bring in management consultants in order to get the loan. The consultants laid out a tired and typical marketing plan to expand the brand but it did not fit the core values or culture. As part of the finance structure, there was $100K to advertise the consultants plan. Jacobs got the loan, and then fired the consultants. Rather than following the canned business plan, they threw the largest outdoor party ever held in Boston. Now that strategy drew national attention and has morphed into huge annual fundraisers giving away millions to their community.

I tell this story because by sticking to core values, Jacobs catapulted the brand into international attention, and built a company that is remarkable and unique. Could he have followed the Madison Avenue marketing strategy and grew his company? Probably, but it would not likely have become the unique worldwide brand it is now. In building destination communities, the core values can vary according to their specific resources and appropriate subcultures. In order to succeed as values continue to shift, however, it is important for all of us to include creating opportunities for real connection and belonging with others, with nature, and with the authentic quality of place in our core values.

Destination Community And In-Migration

One key benefit of creating a tourism destination community can be the creation of a major tool in the attraction of in-migration to the region. In-migration brings huge economic growth opportunities when the retired population and second home-owners move into an area. This can often be the largest economic development driver in a tourism region. One of the biggest impacts both in revenue generation and in livability issues is the in-migration into the area for business opportunities, vacationing, and retirement.

The in-migrated population brings in disposable income that was created outside the region to be spent in the local tourism economy. This creates construction jobs, service jobs, and opportunities for many types of entrepreneurial endeavors. Relocation brings a working population to the region attracted by these new opportunities created by the non-working in-migration populations. This creates conditions for new or expanded local businesses.

Studying the trends in the retirement and second home is an industry onto itself. Housing opportunities for in-migration vary greatly. These may be in master planned communities, downtown infill, or in preexisting traditional neighborhoods. It is a natural companion to studies in tourism. The post recession values of America trend to building an authentic lifestyle. In building a strong destination community, wouldn't you rather seek to draw individuals engaged by the authentic resources you offer to citizens rather than simply processing transient consumers through your region? You create a lifestyle not entertainment. If you are seen as a disposable one-time visit, you will be treated as such. If you attract people that love your story, your subcultures and resources; they will invest into the community. People take care of and protect what they love.

—

Social Hint

Why is it helpful to see from a social point of view?

There are three reasons that it would be helpful for us to look at the community building from another lens, the social (or sociological) perspective, for example. David says that our business is a people business. What he means is that, to build a community, we need to be good at work *with* people, from setting up your team to engaging your clients. I agree with David, but I also know that he is talking from an entrepreneurs point of view seeking to satisfy the true needs of people. I say, our business is to work *for* people, from a social or sociology point of view. No matter if it is our team member, business partners or clients, residents, tourists and visitors, we are all people; we probably assumed or will assume these different roles at different times of our lives.

I believe that understanding people in a society helps us understand our business. Sociology is the study of the people in society and social groups made up by people. There are various scales of sociological discussions, from macro (social groups) to micro (individuals, families). For community building, we will be looking at a range between medium (between micro to macro scale) to macro scale.

1.

The social perspective helps us to think more objectively and critically. Many of us are dedicated to our profession and geographical location, because over the years, we develop emotional bonds with what we do and where we work. It is widely accepted that if we lived in several places and worked in various positions, we tend to become more open minded, thinking with reference and in context. Often, patterns merge in front of our eyes, rather than simply seeing an incident by itself and assuming the uniqueness of it. We also tend to think twice before getting dictated by other people's thinking, in other words, we analyze.

Sociologists, like other social scientists, develop theories and ways of thinking based on large quantity of samples. We study sociology and use it to become open-minded and think more objectively and critically. We don't have to exhaust ourselves living in so many places and see examples personally to come up with the patterns.

For example, historically, every time there is a major social change caused by value shift, there is a shift in people's lifestyle. There is a change in the form of their habitat, from village to town and to major cities, in the western and non-western world likewise. To think objectively, the social change and value shift and the alteration of our way of living that we experienced is not that random or unique. It happened to China 2000 years ago, and happened to the US 200 years ago. This helps us appreciate the context of these changes.

New urbanism and smart growth are hot terms and emerging trends these days. Is this just another trend as what is the trendy color for the next season for the fashion industry or are there truly rational reasons to this trend? What is the driving force behind this trend, if any? So many people are used to repeating what others say without truly thinking why is it this way; and if it is right or wrong. Sociology is closely tied to our profession; it provides a path for us to think objectively and critically.

2.

The social perspective helps us adopt a broader under-standing of our profession and look at the big picture. This involves two angles: horizontally and vertically. What I mean by horizontal is broader understanding that build-ing a tourism community is interdisciplinary by nature; so many other fields are touching and effecting what we do.

Adopting a sociological point of view can be the first step to make us aware of the spectrum of the relevant fields and way of thinking. On the other hand, sociology studies people; it helps us view our profession vertically. We study what people want and what works for people; we can analyze what we did wrong in the past, predict what may happen in the future, and realize something that is trendy may not truly be the best solution in a specific situation.

This book is about tourism and in-migration; precisely, building tourism destination community. By specifying this, we accept the unique social features of these types of communities. Fully aware of this, we explore what works only for this type of community and what is likely to be generalized for other types of communities. We work on our own community, but don't lose sight of who should work with us, what happened in the past, and what may happen in the future.

3.

The social perspective helps our business. The bottom line is that if something holds value over time, economic value for example, then there must be a reason. Gener-ally, values are categorized on three levels of time rang-es, based on human's life span: instant gratification (what works right now), for mid-range return (what will work in a few years given the current trend), or for long term sustainable reasons (looking at reputation in decades or even generations). Thinking from a sociological point of view, we educate ourselves what makes instant gratification, what works for people for their short-term goal, and what meets the needs of the current and possibly the next generations. For example, the cookie cutter formula community is a model that has proven to sell for decades. If we want to sell instant gratification, we can simply copy what has worked, and surely some people will buy into it, regardless if they truly satisfied or not.

If we want to seek return in a few years, we acknowledge that the millennial generation choose to pursue higher education and are starting families later (in late twenties or in their thirties). We also have the empty-nest boomer generation, who downsize their houses as their households become smaller. They may choose to relocate and enjoy their lives in a different location, thus becoming in-migrants to the host communities. Realizing we have these two generations with demands of smaller square footage residents, we can expect to harvest return from building smaller housing with creative floor plans.

Take another step further, if we want to invest in a community that brings long term prosperity, we need to do more work thinking sociologically. The founders of sociology, Auguste Comte and Emile Durkeim, suggested that society is becoming more complex; with highly diverse roles in the society, who depend on each other in social function. Yet our society is also becoming more independent, in terms of emotional ties and social bonds. That being said, for society to maintain stable, building and maintaining strong social bonds between people is critical (sociologists call this social solidarity).

Having this knowledge in mind, we realize for a community to work long term we need to promote and support two things: diversity of social roles which makes up the complexity of the society, and a sense of bond between people to prevent our community from fracturing (see Figure 9). The next step is how to facilitate these two things, through hardware (physical amenities) and software (various social and human capitals, activity programming and identifying complementary subcultures).

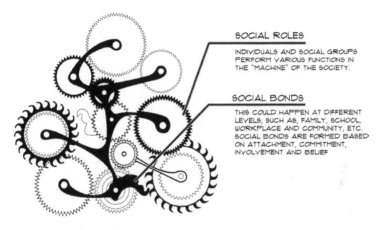

SOCIAL ROLES

INDIVIDUALS AND SOCIAL GROUPS PERFORM VARIOUS FUNCTIONS IN THE "MACHINE" OF THE SOCIETY.

SOCIAL BONDS

THIS COULD HAPPEN AT DIFFERENT LEVELS, SUCH AS, FAMILY, SCHOOL, WORKPLACE AND COMMUNITY, ETC. SOCIAL BONDS ARE FORMED BASED ON ATTACHMENT, COMMITMENT, INVOLVEMENT AND BELIEF

Figure 9: *A diagram of the social complexity of community*

In the following chapters, these points will be expanded and explained from not only the business point of view through observations and examples, but also analyzed from the sociological perspective. I will use several concepts from classic sociologic theory; such as function vs. conflict aspect of a community, social groups and social evolution, and symbolic meanings in the destination communities, to analyze the tourism destination community.

—

Chapter Summary

- The post-recession shift in market values opens greater opportunity for supplying authentic experiences appropriate to the place.

- The market is now fragmented into highly specific areas of interest.
- Generic is not a functional strategy.
- You must define the core values of the community.
- You are building authentic lifestyle that attracts like valued individuals.
- In-migration is a part of successful destination communities and must be planned.
- The value of experiences is overtaking the value of exclusivity.
- You have a specific market; you are not trying to attract everyone.
- The authentic local has become the exotic.
- What is exciting about the post-recession community industry is that there is no longer a tried and true formula for creating these destinations.

Chapter 2

CREATING AUTHENTIC TOURISM DESTINATION COMMUNITIES

M y philosophy for a destination community is that if visiting, living in, and working in the community is not enjoyable, no one will care about the place. We want everyone, visitors, residents, and the workforce to enjoy every experience, activity, interaction, conversation, and perception. We want our colleagues, coworkers, and ourselves to feel that they are doing meaningful work and understand how what we do is important to creating the experience and lifestyle.

Sure, the tourist experience is fun on occasion. But to attract quality growth in a region that will value and protect the assets and traditions important to place; the ultimate visitor experience is a sense of belonging that creates a protective attitude about a place. In other words, people want to find their tribe, not simply to be a tourist. To do this we must create a community of belonging for our visitors, residents and coworkers.

We must create an atmosphere of personal growth and a culture of helping others. Hedonism is a nice place to visit but we all know the rest of that phrase. It can be fun for short periods of time but it is not a sustainable or fulfilling lifestyle. More and more research on the hedonic treadmill theory clearly shows that the conspicuous status seeking that many communities

19

marketed successfully for many years is breaking down as the prevalent value proposition for in-migration decisions. The industry so permeated a calibrated idea of the American dream that the expectation of the masses was that these stereotypes would make them happy. Now isolation is one of the top problems facing communities of all types.

Quality of Experience and Quality of Life

The wonderful thing about our business is that having a successful product means giving our residents and visitors a better quality of life. Quality of life and experience must be core products for a tourism system to be sustainable in a community. Communities, like people, develop a character. Part of our leadership responsibility is to help shape and bring out that character into a positive and vibrant place that gives a good return on investment. What a potential resident is looking for in a community varies more today than at any time in the past. For example, sporting communities have become authentic options in a world where the transient nature of our careers have moved us many times from the land we knew and understood in childhood.

Today people want a more holistic experience, yet still based on their values of place. In order to be successful in the destination community market, you must be good at what you do, authentic, relevant, and specific. It could be the arts or foodie culture for example. Regardless of being arts, equestrian, hiking, fishing, or any activity authentic to your location, you must have the knowledge and be a serious believer in the lifestyle you advocate. Your people must fall within the vernacular of the lifestyle vision. You need to find the people that believe in the inherent value and vision of your community. They are your tribe. Being a one size fits all will not attract your tribe. It lacks vision and specificity. These are the Obsessed. They are not generic; they are individuals that have chosen to excel in a chosen passion. They don't believe in half measures when it comes to their passion. However, if you can service the needs and satisfy the values of the true believer, you will attract the Interested and the Random. I will explain more on this in chapter 3.

The cultures of destination lifestyles wanted are varied. The new urbanism, conservation ruralism, big city life, small town life, the mountain, beach or lake lifestyles, tennis, golf, sporting, boat in, fly in, and equestrian are just a few of the amenity rich lifestyles vying for attention in their specific market. While quality of life and experience is impacted by the quality of amenities and maintenance, these things are minimum standards that are easy to benchmark. The core of quality of life, regardless of a community's lifestyle theme, is more intangible but can be equally impacted by our leadership.

Sense of community is one of the intangible indicators of the quality of life and experience in a destination community. Building a sense of community is about personal growth and social interaction. Too often governing entities stop at providing facilities and take little responsibility beyond that point. Building a sense of community, and providing opportunities for individual growth and support of chosen lifestyle are essential to building quality of life for the residents and visitors. People want to feel their lives are being well spent.

Just as people evolve to focus on human needs higher on Maslow's Hierarchy, our design of place both from the physical and psychological viewpoint must seek to serve the higher purposes. I use Maslow's Hierarchy as a key planning element in both tourism development and destination community design. We must always seek to create places that create conditions conducive to individual growth and creativity, which is my interpretation of enlightenment or self actualization.

Corporate Monoculture vs. Complementary Subcultures

As I have the opportunity to speak to many groups, I find there is often a misunderstanding of the types of tourism systems and the degrees to which tourism should play a role in the economic development of a community. To build the economic development benefits of tourism while retaining the livability and character of a region, I am constantly promoting the development of destination systems using the authentic natural assets and vernacular of the region. There is often a general low-grade fear of how tourism will impact a community. To understand the difference between types of destination systems, it is important to look at the basics of how they develop. While there are always exceptions in destinations, I have found the majority use one of two models: the corporate monoculture or the complementary subcultures (see Figure 10).

In a corporate monoculture, we typically are setting a formalized stage for entertainment. It may be participatory entertainment but it is corporately structured. Monoculture developers usually want to find a blank slate to build the vision upon. These corporate monocultures typically impose their model upon an area rather than enhance the pre-existing culture. In the worst cases, the monoculture may overwhelm and obliterate the authentic subcultures that pre-existed the development. Examples of these are the development surrounding monoculture attractions such as Vegas or the Disney properties. There will be peripheral service business development such as hotels, restaurants, and side activities but they still support the single narrative. Very narrow but clear expectations are set.

On the other hand, with community-based tourism, we wish to enhance the organically occurring subcultures. Take the North Carolina High Country as an example, where the fly-fishing, golf, mountain biking, climbing, folk arts, and skiing subcultures all coexist to support and be supported by a vibrant culinary, music, and retail economy that adds to the livability of the region. Tourism development through complimentary sub-cultures creates opportunities for passion based entrepreneurs and small businesses with a relatively low barrier for entry. It also enhances and protects livability.

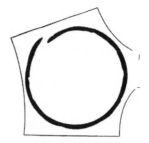

A CORPORATE MONOCULTURE
BREAKS THE ORIGINALLOCAL CULTURE.

COMPLEMENTARY SUBCULTURES
RESPECT, PROTECT AND PRESERVE THE
ORIGINAL LOCAL CULTURE WHILE
ADDING NEW ENERGY.

Figure 10 : *The different impact of monoculture model vs. subculture model on original local culture*

In a monoculture, there is one narrative to give the user an understanding of how they will structure their visit due to the narrow brand control. There is nothing wrong with single attraction tourism in the correct setting. This can be very beneficial in creating opportunity for support business development - chain hotels, retail, and restaurants. It can also have the effect of concentrating tourism dollars by creating many lower paying corporate jobs while the profits leave the community. However, it is the big fish that many tourism developers seek as it falls into the corporate realm not the more complex "Handmade" realm. It can force out the original population by destroying the historic economies and lifestyles. Therefore, for the vast majority of small towns and rural areas, fostering a tourism economy based of complimentary subcultures is far more doable, preferable, and controllable than the monoculture option. Arts, heritage, nature based, sporting, and adventure are just a few of the many types of destinations being created. My point is, destinations are becoming ever more unique and celebrate individualism while promoting and protecting a specific culture.

Handmade Community and Its Subcultures

Handmade destination community building is a people business. It is intensely local and personal. It is very entrepreneurially oriented. It celebrates individualism. It draws creative types: artists and performers, athletes and philosophers, poets and farmers. To use an intentional oxymoron, there are several categories of individuals that are involved with handmade tourism. Some are your authentic homegrown tourism assets. Others start as your visitors and often your residents. We need to understand these classifications see how a subculture builds community.

This can be challenging in the rural / small town setting. If it were easy, every place would do it. While it is these traditions and lifestyles that create the potential for handmade tourism, there can also be regional and business practices that hinder destination development. One of the easiest mistakes that we make in trying to create a destination service system is taking the wrong point of view. It is not about us, except to the extent that it is our passions that are attractive to a market and we would like to maximize the socio-economic benefits of serving it. For example, in the South, many small town businesses and resident based communities close their doors and roll up the streets on late afternoons and evenings. This makes servicing a destination market difficult. To look at building destination/tourism based economic development, we must educate our business environment by showing the opportunities to serve this new market.

Not only do we have to be open and available for visitors, but also we have to understand that the subcultures and values are the reasons our visitors come. We must always focus on conveying the sincere and authentic culture of the region in the point view of the target market. There is a myriad of subculture activities that can be the core draw (see Figure 11), but in all cases people come to have an enjoyable time – enjoyment is our deliverable regardless of discipline. In other words, the markets visiting these destinations are doing so because of an interest in the passions of the sub-cultures.

Figure 11: *Little River Blueway is a destination context region, featuring outdoor adventures for its visitors and residents. (Logo Concepts by David Twiggs and Kirk Smith)*

In looking at how to grow handmade tourism destination, there is no need to worry about trying to satisfy a vast array of all potential interests. You are not trying to attract everyone; instead you want those visitors and new residents that appreciate the authentic culture of your community. Be who you are. That being said, if you are going to create the conditions to draw other people's money; you must deal with other people. As with any economic driver, there will be impacts on the community. With poor planning, infrastructure and support systems growth could possibly ruin the resources that add the value. This is not sustainable. This is not planned economic development and smart growth. Proper planning and growth control are vital to retain the true flavor and livability of the region. You must know what level of growth is enough and build in the controls, lest you kill the goose. This will be unpacked in detail in a later chapter.

I hesitate to put one my favorite places into a book but the Town of Saluda, in the Green River region of North Carolina, is a good example. Complementary subcultures centering on a key natural feature, the gorge and the river in this case, spins off many opportunities. World class whitewater kayaking is a core lifestyle activity focusing on the Narrows for the obsessed, the Upper and Lower sections for the interested and random. Trout fishing opportunities for all levels are throughout the region. Hiking and biking abound. The obsessed set the tone for the region. The interested group supports the local outfitters with instruction on quality whitewater boats, standup paddleboards and rubber kayaks. The random supply has a market on the lower section with thousands of tubers floating the river supporting several tubing outfitters and campgrounds. It has an understandable story. It is easy for me to quickly have a picture in my head of what my experience there will be like. If I were not interested in the complimentary subcultures the area services, I would not be satisfied with my visit but more likely I just would not have come. You would have also wasted any money spent on trying to get your story in front of me. We don't have money to waste. Target your market.

Visitors, who come for hiking, biking, zip lines and climbing mix well with those that simply come to enjoy the natural beauty and walk the quaint streets of Appalachian heritage. With this visitor base, the approximately 5.2-acre downtown commercial core of Saluda, population of 711, has the opportunity for supplying more diverse activities and support services. The general stores, green markets, and B&B's are prime features. Several cafes and specialty restaurants are supported. My favorite restaurant is "The Purple Onion." Its concept value was creating a sustainable venue for a vibrant live music scene for many local and regional musicians. To do this they created an outstanding eclectic restaurant to support this goal. Art shops, spa services, and ice cream stores round out some of the other peripheral services. All in support of and supported by the sub-cultures visiting the area.

All this is in a tight sustainable setting that seeks to protect the nature of the community and the natural resources that draw the visitors as a base for exploring the region. So far, they seem to have put controls in place to control growth: they seem to know when enough is enough and have protected the very things that make them attractive. It was economic development but not at any cost. This makes Saluda an example of good planning so the area reaps the benefits of a tourism / destination community economy while remaining sustainable, livable and protective of their traditions and culture.

Slow Culture

Wendell Berry describes what I call slow culture in his talk on Natural Gifts. He said, "Certain things you learn simply because you happen to be on hand, you couldn't have planned to learn it. It is like questions you have about the local neighborhood, they're hard to remember when you are with the person you want to ask, so finally the conversation will come around and you will be reminded. I have thought of this sometimes as the pattern of reminding although I am not sure that it's a pattern. But in local conversation, in local experience, over an extended period of time, certain themes will be played and replayed again, and learning is more a matter of being on hand than it is of establishing a curriculum."

I focus on creating cultures of belonging. Experiencing a culture has many degrees: the spectator experience, the educational experience, the deeper understanding of belonging. People want to find their tribe rather than a transient entertainment based culture that has been fostered by many destinations and master planned communities. A model for rural economic development is building systems that foster access to the organic slow culture of a region based on the true subcultures and natural assets. That may be recreational, arts, agrarian, sporting, craftsman or conservation, but it is a slow culture. It took time to develop and time to enter. Allowing access to experience the authentic culture of our community, not simply the consumer-based entertainment, creates a place to experience belonging, learning, and growth that has last relevance and value (see Figure 12). If it is a readymade, generic or inauthentic culture, no one will invest the energy because there is nothing real to belong to.

Figure 12: Kids enjoying the entertaining and education experience in the nature through paddling and kayaking (photo by author)

Connection to Place

Janis Joplin, the famous singer-songwriter of 1960's and 70's, once said that America should be looking for sincerity and a good time. To me, that falls into my philosophy that a community must be focused on being a collection of real relationships rather than simply a defined real estate space. The consumer and hedonistic based stereotypes are breaking down in favor of meaningful involvement and service. That is for all; the residents, visitors, and those that work in these communities.

In a country of transient jobs, corporate transfers, and instant communities, there is often isolation or disconnection. Finding a place that one can truly connect and build real relationships is a core of in migration. A person visits as a tourist because they have an attraction to subcultures of the area. Ideally, they feel a connection, a potential belonging, to a place. Local relationships forge when visitors begin to spend more time, take on additional skills and develop bonds in a chosen subculture. As a result, this fosters deeper and more authentic experiences. More time is invested; from visitor to part time to full time residency is established – a new local is born. There are people that want your authentic product. Find them, don't try to trick the masses, only to disappoint them and work your tail off to service low yield disinterested customers lured under false pretenses. In other words, be more of what you already want to be. Again, you are not trying to attract everyone in the world, just those that are interested in your specific subcultures.

Without connection to place, economic development can take place but it will not necessarily be in harmony with the nature of the greater community. Over 25 years prior to the recent recession, as a nation, we fell into a value standard that celebrated material wealth and consumption as status indicators. This went so far as to celebrate the workaholic, the over scheduled and those that sacrificed personal relationships to create that wealth. There were many destinations and master planned communities developed with celebrating wealth as the standard. Just as we know money is not the key to happiness, attracting wealth is not the key to sustainable communities or livable destination economies. A focus on wealth only is purely quantitative and tends to not create more "locals" but creates a "them" class that has an inauthentic lifestyle superimposed over the landscape with little consideration of local culture. That doesn't mean that the visitor and new residents you attract will not be wealthy. They most likely will be or they would not have had the resources to live where they want or purchase a second home. They are not coming to display their wealth; they are coming because they want to be part of your lifestyle. My point is, it is not the old style celebration of excess that is the key attractor but the opportunity to belong to an authentic subculture. Now people are people and you may always have a bit of us/them mindset, but it will be drastically reduced if you start with a better value proposition. Borrowing again from Wendell Berry's thoughts in his interview on Natural Gifts make to my point: if we change the standard from drawing wealth to creating health, we are looking at a different model.

Health and Wellbeing

At a 2013 Urban Land Institute meeting, Peter Rummell, who was instrumental in the development of the St. Joe communities in Florida, predicted wellness as the key community development theme over the next 20 years. As opposed to the prerecession conspicuous consumption development model, health is a more complex value objective. This shift in the value proposition was already happening with destinations such as Balsam Mountain Preserve, Tryon Farms, Homestead Preserve, Serenbe, etc. Wendell Berry, the American novelist, poet, environmental activist, cultural critic, and farmer, referenced Alan Ereira's *The Heart of the World,* highlighting a perspective on wellness from the Kogi tribe of Sierra Nevada in Columbia,

South America. Berry stated, "Health involves others, other things, the place that you take your life from…it is of course in part physical health but physical health does not exist apart from the health of other things. Health ultimately involves the community, and the community ultimately involves the place and the natural life of that place so that real health is a balanced life: a life in harmony with your immediate physical environment. So nothing is left out of health because health always implies wholeness… being right with your local place, your community and your household; that job proposes many little jobs of work and some big ones."

So how do we build communities where we place health and wellness with our immediate world as the standard? The answer is to develop the authentic nature of the community. If you develop and expand upon the authentic nature of the community, the natural quality of place, and design your built environment in harmony with the natural assets everything becomes your amenity. For many years the development model was simply locating a place to drop in the standard formula community model. The banks, builders and marketers understood this model. Profits were predictable and a proliferation system was in place to replicate this basic community design. It was marketed to a transient professional population that was accustomed to a certain level of disconnection and looking for instant community. This created a lot of "us" vs. "them" mentalities. We can see many examples of thousands of unremarkable communities failing because the formula design was overlaid on areas with little or no natural quality of place.

This does not mean that you should not have traditional amenities offered as part of your development plan; they can add tremendous value in the right circumstances. However, relevant communities do not simply rely on the gates and golf courses. It simply means that the value creation is from creating the conditions for healthy lifestyle balance. It means designing in a way to enhance the natural quality of place, rather than inflicting a common model over the physical environment. In destination development, looking at community integration with the nature of the region is the key.

—

Social Hint

The function vs. conflict side of a community

There are two main concept streams of thought when we look at the structure of a society: function theory and conflict theory. We can look at the quality of life and authentic experience from both of these theories. Function theory says the society is composed by people functioning in different areas, like organs on a living body, to support the growth of a society. Conflict theory states that the society, made by individuals and social groups, is constantly in the competition for limited resources. I think function theory presents the emphasis on the cooperation side while the conflict theory is interested in the exclusivity of participation in certain activities in the society. So does enjoying a higher quality of life and authentic experience in a tourism destination community show the function side or conflict side of the society? I say it is both.

Let's talk about the conflict side, which is also the exclusivity side of the story. As David talked about in the first chapter, since the 1950's, the social value is becoming more and more detached from the agrarian life style. Wealth allowed living a different experience, such as grocery shopping in a supermarket, driving luxury cars, living in a suburban house. It was the new concept that quickly became the "American Dream." In the mid to late 20th century, that is what people were after, with more and more people getting qualified to the "sophisticated" lifestyle. When this model of sophistication was first identified in the American society, only a small wealthy portion of society was able to realize their American Dream; while others were still struggling to get away from the agrarian lifestyle. That is exclusion: whenever there is something considered advanced, there is exclusion. Being qualified to this smaller portion of people shows a socially viewed prestige. Now that this social value in the parts of America's society is going through a shift in the recent years, many realize the classic "American Dream" cannot give them true fulfillment. More of them are now choosing to seek authentic experiences and return to the understanding of integration with the natural world.

David's thoughts on building an authentic tourism destination caters to this awakening, and therefore it is advanced thinking in our current time. However, inevitably there will only be a certain group of people who can afford this new lifestyle: they first need to find this specific lifestyle appealing (emotional attraction); second, they need to be able to afford to travel, relocate or purchase a second home (social freedom, time and financial situation). To this "exclusivity", David gives out his views on the solution. Unlike the 'mass marketing of the past. We can reach our specific market.

- People who find the lifestyle appealing – we need to find our own "tribe", and we are not trying to attract everyone.
- People who can afford to travel, relocate or purchase a second home – the in migrant makes a big part of our market. They are mobile; bringing pensions, retirements, or abilities to work where they please. The authentic nature of the region will bring people who have the professional skills and cultural understanding to be a good fit in the local destination community

economy.

This is very much aligned with Maslow's hierarchy of human needs (see Figure 13). Being provided with basic physical shelter and necessary utility, people can survive. When a community is merely keeping up the physical infrastructure condition, and not paying attention to the functionality and social value, people will move out as soon as they become financially better-off. If a place is diligent about the physical maintenance and it happens to be at a convenient location, but the update on social value is neglected, then it will attract people that are ignoring their own higher human needs. People will move out as soon as they find a place they feel they belong better. Only when a community takes care and keeps all three aspects updated, will it grow, thrive, and have a longer life cycle.

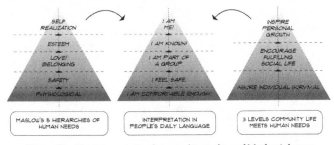

Figure 13 : The interpretation between hierarchies of Maslow's human needs and 3-tier criteria for communities

On the other hand, the functional aspect of the community is worth looking at. For a community to truly function as a community, we need our people to enjoy their visit or residence in that community; both the solitude and the communal side of the community life. This is what we call the "sense of community." This sense of community is vital for any community to survive. Who wants to live in a place where they dislike each other and do not feel connected by the values of their community? In sociology, this sense of community contributes to the "solidarity" or "stability," of a community or society. According to the funders of sociology, Auguste Comte and Emile Durkheim, the society is evolving, from simple and to more complex. For example, before the industrial revolution, most population lived agrarian lifestyle in the rural environment. When the convenience comes with the mass production and the freedom of labor from farming duties, people start to assume new occupations and choose unconventional lifestyles for the times. This adds to the complexity of the society.

As the society evolves, its functions begin to change from "mechanic solidarity" to "organic solidarity". Mechanic solidarity is when people assume similar yet simpler functions in the society; people are more self-sufficient, yet are more emotionally dependent on each other. For example, in a rural village where each family farms and produces their own food and they watch out for each other. Organic solidarity happens when the society becomes more complex. People take on functions in vastly diverse fields: people greatly depend on each other to get basic services yet they are more emotionally independent from each other. For example, an IT person living in the bay area of California needs to call food delivery to his office. So for this to happen, people from many professions are involved: the farms, transportation sector, processors, food purchasing, chef, and food delivery person. When he makes the phone call, the phone company is involved. The city street, office building, every step on this simple scenario implies that there are people involved. It is not likely this IT guy has a personal relationship with any of these people that make his meal in the office happen. In this background, the mindset of individualism is fostered.

The wisdom in the monoculture versus complementary subculture model in tourism destination community as David proposed, is that it acknowledges that society is becoming more and more complex, and "one size fits all" models will not work well in today's society. People now have the freedom to choose different kinds of interests, hobbies, and lifestyles. Complementary subculture model appreciates this sense of individualism and provides the options.

As complementary subculture model makes more sense than monocultural model, it is extremely important for the destination community to deliberately create opportunities for the interest groups to mix and bond and prevent the community from fracturing.

—

Chapter Summary

- The wonderful thing about our business is that having a successful product means giving our residents and visitors a better quality of life than they would have without us.
- We must create an atmosphere of personal growth and a culture of helping others.
- You must be good at what you do; authentic, relevant and specific.
- To build the economic benefits of tourism while retaining the livability and character of a region, use the authentic assets and vernacular of the region.
- In complimentary subcultures, we typically focus on creating a system for belonging rather than entertainment.
- Tourism development through complimentary subcultures creates opportunities for passion based entrepreneurs and small businesses.
- Destinations are becoming more unique and celebrate individualism while promoting and protecting their

specific cultures.
- Handmade destination community building is intensely local and personal.
- Know what level of growth is enough, build controls, lest you kill the goose.
- Finding a place that one can truly connect and build real relationships is a core of in-migration.
- The value creation is creating the conditions for healthy lifestyle balance in your unique place.
- Be more of what you already want to be.

Chapter 3

UNDERSTANDING HUMAN CAPITAL IN SUBCULTURES: CELEBRATING INDIVIDUALISM

No one is doing what everyone else is. I think I would be about the average person based on my demographics: white male coming of age in a southern college town in the early 1980's. One generation off the cattle farm, I grew up on traditional field sports, rock and roll liberally mixed with blue-grass music. You would think I would be right in the middle of the class but there is no class anymore.

I think I am typical, yet why don't I fit into that old mass marketing mold? Hardly anyone does anymore. Twenty years ago you could rely on my cohort to be watching one of two things on TV on a Thursday night. There was just not much choice. We listened to the same two radio stations and read the same magazines. You could make a couple of easy advertising investments and put your message in front of most of us.

Today I get the news that I am interested in tweeted to me directly from specific online sources. I don't watch television in the traditional sense. I stream only the shows I want and have not seen a traditional commercial in years. There is no channel guide or schedule in my life. I don't have cable and gladly pay to stream my favorite radio station, which is from several states away. The print material I do faithfully follow; Garden and Gun, Covertside, Gray's Sporting Journal, Modern Farmer, and Fast

Company are so niche specific that only those that have an insider position dare to advertise.

We can find our interests so specifically; we have no need to be generalist. Seth Godin, an American author, entrepreneur, marketer, and public speaker, said there is no longer an American canon of materials that we can reliably expect to be common knowledge. We have an unlimited supply of media but can laser focus on our interests only and tune out the noise of the advertising machine. This specificity, along with the mobility of Americans means we do not have to live in a generic place and take our chances that we will find our "people." Today we can just go on Meet Up and find a group that shares an affinity for eclectic banjo covers of baroque composers or whatever your weird interest may be. Generic is dead. Average is dead. Compromising to the least offensive denominator is dead. Celebrate the unique!

Complementary Subcultures Celebrate the Individual

In complimentary subcultures, we are typically focusing on creating a system for belonging. Our destination should be a place I aspire to belong to. This aspiration is created by exposure to the human capital of the subculture. With community based tourism we wish to enhance or be more of what we already want to be. Your target market aspires to be part of your subculture. It becomes passion driven rather than utilitarian system. You don't need a cashier. You need a cashier that gathers a crowd because she is telling the story of her last rock-climbing, golf or scuba diving outing. Remember you are not marketing to everyone in the world. We need only attract those who are passionate about what we authentically are or can be.

Kevin Kelly, a co-founder of Wired Magazine and author, puts forth the concept of "1000 True Fans" on his website, kk.org. To use his concepts in our tourism setting, a "true fan" cares deeply about your specific subculture. They will go out of their way to support your system. They will introduce you to others. Seth Godin explains that a "true fan" brings three others with them to your system. These visitors fall into my "interested" category. They are not yet the Obsessed "true fan" but they will spend much more time and money than the random uninterested visitor. They are much easier to find and target than the random visitor. The random are fine. They come for many different reasons. We welcome them, embrace them and try to make them feel the belonging. However, we will not spend our limited marketing dollars trying to attract the random. True fans connect with and create other true fans. They expand your voice in explaining your integrated tourism system.

There is nothing wrong with single attraction tourism. It is the big fish that many tourism developers seek. This falls into the corporate realm of tourism development. This can be very beneficial or it can have the homogenizing effect of concentrating tourism dollars creating many, but low paying corporate jobs while the big dollars leave the community. There are not many of these instant fixes out there so I don't concentrate on them. Handmade destination communities are much more doable.

A key benefit to lifestyle/subculture based tourism systems is the attraction of more people who love what you are. Visitors that deeply care about the culture and environment of the area in which they carry out their recreational activity often relocate or buy vacation homes there. These become even more assets if fostered. In more corporate/entertainment based tourism economies this is not the case. Do you really ever plan to live outside the gates of Disneyworld or move to Vegas? Would you want your town turning into that type of environment? Some may, but this book does not focus on the corporate tourism development.

Human Capital: Who are your people?

Handmade Tourism is a people business. I have found it to

be very entrepreneurially oriented. It celebrates individualism. Draws creative types, artists and performers. It draws sportsmen and women, philosophers, poets and farmers. There is space for chefs, musicians, and artists to thrive. In many cases there is a relatively low barrier for entry for many tourism operations. To use an intentional oxymoron again, there are several categories of individuals that are involved with handmade tourism. Some become homegrown tourism assets. Others become your visitors and often your residents. We need to understand these classifications be able to identify individuals in our communities that fall into these categories (also see Figure 14).

- The Obsessed
- The Interested
- The Random

THE OBSESSED
—

Many of our passions are such because they bring us to focus on the "now " and are aimed for some type of physical or spiritual growth. Some of this is a type of meditation or contemplative practice that brings us to an appreciation of now. Not dwelling in the past or worrying the future. While relaxation is part of our leisure goals, we rarely want to spend all our time in a soporific state. We more often seek a balance to create the peak flow experience. Mihaly Czikszentmihaly, in his TED Talk (http://www.ted.com) based on his book *Flow: The Psychology of Optimal Experience* asks, "What makes a life worth living?" He goes on to explain that engagement in activities that challenge and allow us to grow creates a state of "flow." It is focused motivation. Time passes unnoticed, as we are enthralled in an activity we are passionate about. This idea can also be seen in Maslow's earlier work on peak experience. I call people who base their lifestyle choices on seeking this "flow," the *Obsessed*.

Handmade tourism creates skills and knowledge based relationships. Yes, many people that relocate to your destination may be wealthy. That is the nature of second homes. The obsessed may be rich or poor. They have self selected to be part of a group that values passion and experience over simple wealth. These folks are your key human capital. They set the tone for the destination community. It doesn't matter if your community is focusing on arts, outdoors, history, or any number of subcultures. It is the obsessed in these groups that should be used. They are both your ambassadors and your primary target market.

THE INTERESTED
—

Once you have organized your subcultures of the Obsessed into a representative brand, your marketing focuses on those complimentary subcultures. While you are targeting them you also draw a group I call the *Interested.* This group tends to have a general knowledge of your core activities and is interested in exploring the lifestyle further. They may be active in a similar subculture. The Interested identify with the subculture and want to learn and belong. Creating a destination culture that allows for participation beyond the Obsessed is key to moving beyond a great hidden asset into a successful destination community. If you are remarkable, these people will tell others.

THE RANDOM
—

These folks happened upon you. They may be visiting relatives, on business, or just curious after hearing about you. We don't spend resources trying to attract this group. However never lose an opportunity. If your destination is understandable and memorable, you may have generated a future person to move into the Interested category and generated future visits to your destination.

My Personal Case Study

In my family, riding to hounds or foxhunting is our sporting tradition and flow experience. We enjoy many traditional field sports such as quail and duck hunting; but hunting hounds is the avocation that focuses the family energy and dictates the daily lifestyle. We have been fortunate to be fully involved in training hounds, whelping, and walking out puppies as well as whipping in on hunting days.

It is of no tangible value to hurl yourself and a twelve hundred pound horse though narrow rutted trails over a ditches and fences at full gallop simply to hear the voices of the hounds. There is no trophy, we are not out to kill anything; nor is there a winner declared at the end of the day. It is simply the total immersion in the "now." My wife who is obsessed with the care, training and general happiness of the hounds calls this total focus on the "now" Kairos time or God's Time. Total flow.

To those who participate in obsession activities, there is time spent in contemplative almost meditative state. It also has times of physiological levels of stress response that make us feel exhilarated and alive. I describe one element of mounted foxhunting as a focused nature meditation. Actually, having your mind and body completely tuned in on every sound, smell, and movement in the forest and rivers, every shift in the breeze, and even feeling the changes in barometric pressure and ionization of the air. Each of these refines your consciousness of the moment. This is what ancient cultures called being in rhythm with nature, not in rhythm to the clock and schedules of chronos time. This allows the meandering of your brain synapses though the collection of experiences, knowledge and the unconsciously received signals from nature. This culminates into intuition and ideas where we are in tune and engrossed in the "now." The contemplative part of Kairos time.

But most obsession activities do not simply strive for a meditative state of mind. A point of commitment is crossed. Beyond this point is only instinct, intuition, physical endurance and gut reaction. That may be that first drop of your ski tips over the steep lip of an untried basin. It may be digging your paddle in to turn your kayak into that technical section of water or setting the hook on a trout. Watch golfers as they physically contort their bodies after the ball is hit trying to will the ball to turn slightly into the green.

The second element to Kairos time in foxhunting is just beyond this Point of Commitment. The physiological stress and pleasure response starts engaging. Adrenaline and dopamine fire up in different areas of the brain. You have been in a meditative state soaking in the natural rhythms, the first hound speaks, then another, then the entire pack smells the scent trail of a coyote. What ensues from here I liken to a combination of a horizontal free-fall on horseback and the abandonment of self-direction to the whims of nature, geography, and landscape. It is primal.

Fear evaporates; you are not even cognizant of your horse. You flow through the countryside instinctively picking your path based on the sound of the running pack. On lucky occasions, you are blessed to run amongst the hounds galloping with the coyote in sight ahead of you but never knowing where the next direction may be. It is not about want you want. There is nothing under your control. You are blessed to be a spectator of an ancient play. The actors are the natural instincts and physicality of the animals and they have been playing out this scene for centuries. The coyote's have superior knowledge of their home area and the hounds drive to follow their scent. I have followed them on circle after circle in one square mile before the coyote ducked back into one of his dens. I have followed them on 16-mile points never making a turn. When that first hound speaks, we do not know what direction we may go, the duration we may run, nor what obstacles we may encounter. We humans are not necessary to the play.

I have experienced this shoulder to shoulder with extremely wealthy individuals and folks that could barely afford the gas to drive out that morning. The point is we all belong based on our abilities and knowledge. The respect of our peers had nothing to do with wealth, position, or anything outside of belonging to this subculture.

Obsession activities are the root activities that can become the basis for strong subculture tourism economies given the proper resources. These activities go beyond the generic attraction activities, restaurants-for example. This is recreation at its root; re-creation. These activities exist purely for the physical and spiritual benefit of the participant. It is the basis to develop the authentic tourism brand. Like rock climbing, mountain biking, expedition, surfing, kayaking, hunting, fishing, equestrian or skiing; these subculture visitors are specialized and expect good conditions for their activity. Beyond the specialized gear and guide businesses they create, these subculture visitors require the same tourism support assets that any other activity does. They need housing, food, provisions, and entertainment. All the same elements that make living in a destination community desirable.

Branding the Obscure

I use foxhunting here as an analogy of how a relatively obscure activity adds to the tourism brand of region. The attraction to the obsessed is obvious. While attracting many visitors year round for hound shows and riding out for hound exercise, the serious foxhunting tradition peaks with the opening meet in early November (see Figure 15). We organize hundreds of visitors into wagons, moving them through miles of farm and forestlands. We organized wagons for those coming without reservations, reserved wagons for busloads of out of town visitors, corporately sponsored wagons for corporations bringing clients and employees furthering their business opportunities. These wagons are loaded down with picnic baskets and ice chests with the provision for a day afield. We even have a special wagon with bathroom facilities following for the visitors' needs.

Figure 15: *The community and visitors gather at the foxhunting event*

After the pageantry of the riders jumping into the grounds surrounded by visitors for the Blessing of the Hounds; the wagons follow a carefully designed route, stopping at preselected vistas for the riders in their traditional attire thundering by. The visitors' sensory experience peaks watching a hundred plus horses jumping fences and galloping after a pack of 50 hounds giving full voice after a scent line that we have carefully laid for the benefit of our audience. This happens repeatedly over the course of the day as visitors enjoy food and cocktails on their wagons while moving through the beautiful countryside. All this culminates just before sunset on Champagne Hill where riders, horses, hounds and visitors enjoy cocktails in the gloaming of the day before riding back to fireside barbeque.

It is talked about long after the event as visitors return home to tell their stories. It attracts the Obsessed, the Interested and the Random. It is a major tourism brand celebration for the area. However, a single event does not make a culture. The authentic foxhunting culture and lifestyle that exists year round that draws visitors and relocation to the region is the true tourism driver. This event simply celebrates an authentic regional lifestyle that is appropriate to the tourism brand. It also fits with the other key regional subcultures such as fishing, hiking, and the historic nature of the area. If an activity as obscure as mounted foxhunting can be such an economic driver for a region, most any region can find a mix of subcultures that are both attracted to your regions assets and become the basis for an authentic destination culture.

Understanding your core tourism customer is very important in natural resource / obsession activity based tourism development. Participants in obsession activities focus their spending and energies on their passions and the environment that allows it. Most people go to work everyday to be able to pay for what we prioritize. We will sacrifice other types of spending if it means not doing all the "normal" things like television, video games, and consumer based lifestyles. We do what is important to us. We often are more emotionally invested in the region where we play than the region where we work. It is where we want our second homes. It is where we want to retire. Why should this type of individual fall in love with your region? What are the benefits to the local community?

RELOCATION

A key economic benefit when done well is people choosing to relocate into the region. This can be a primary or second home. A destination creates opportunities for businesses to start or relocate into the region to become part of the destination assets. This has property tax and sales tax revenue opportunities for the host jurisdiction. As for what draws relocation, we choose to move to an area that supported our subculture along with many complimentary ones. My family and I could have lived anywhere we wished. We settled on an area that had made our subculture a priority in it's branding. In this case, the destination attracted many enthusiastic visitors from the northern United States and Canada for extended rentals and second homes.

These visitors bring a large lodging, rental and second home market with them as well as additional seasonal business for area retailers and restaurants. Many of these visitors now consider the region their second home. This is because there is an authentic subculture lifestyle that fits into the bigger culture of the community. You are attracting a subculture that truly love your natural assets and will seek to protect rather than exploit them.

SPECIALIZE
—

Building a community for the generic average is a failing proposition. We cannot continue creating simple monocultures-we must embrace inter-related layers of complementary subcultures sharing the same natural resource. It could be a tremendous surf break, a beautiful mountain region, or lake system. Different subcultures can love a region for many different reasons. Diverse communities are resilient, listen to the investment gurus, and diversify. Meanwhile, in creating a community, we must build the environment for the specific to thrive. In my experience developing outdoor sports venues, I have always found that if we create the conditions for the expert, the fanatic, the gear head to flourish, the interested amateurs will flock there. These are the people that buy the homes, fill the restaurants and create the demand for services. These folks build community.

It is so easy to find the real. Embrace individuality and the diverse subcultures that share the same love for quality of place. We can find our authentic people living our favored experiences.

Human Capital Is A Key Programming Asset

These are the people that understand how to put on authentic events for each subculture. (see Figure 16). Make it easy for other organizations to create their branded events in your venues. Every subculture has brand leaders and event coordination. You don't rely on someone else to add their share of value to your brand but working with key subculture brand leaders, will greatly enhance your brand. You are creating a narrative for the events coordinators you are seeking to bring into your venues. Focus on the organizer's ease and understanding. Attract the businesses you need, but don't become that business unless it fills a void you cannot fill with a subculture specialist.

A great deal of my work deals with action sports. This is completely intentional because it is the major sporting genre in the minds of Americans, tailing edge Boomers and younger. Jake Schwartz, cofounder of Quicksilver Hotel and Resorts International, recently was on a panel discussion for Urban Land Institute addressing the impact Millennials have on destination development. He made several key points on the importance of action sports genre. There is now about $350 billion spent annually in the action sports industry. Action sports teens influence $200-300 billion of their parent's annual income. These sports are cross-generational and cross-cultural. Action sports are seeing explosive growth, much faster than traditional sports. While many action sports take place in natural settings, the millennial general mindset of "FOMO" or "fear of missing out" make them want to gather at a scene for whatever subculture they choose. Take the success examples of different mountain games such as the Go Pro Mountain Games and the entire Red Bull Branded series of events. Tailing edge boomers and Gen X started this evolution of action sports; the Millennial have never known a world without it.

So why am I not spending much more energy talking about specific programming when I feel it is so important? The subcultures will drive your types of events and programs. Typically amateur event coordinators emerge within your subcultures and will plan the events. You must have enough understanding of the subculture to know what is on their needs list and anticipate general event needs. These "event coordinators" may or may not be an event professional. It could be for those groups wanting meetings and conferences in interesting places. These folks organize the Interested looking for a more entry level subculture experience. However, they tend to want that experience in a very interesting place. That place is usually created by the Obsessed. For the Obsessed, events may be coordinated by a combination on the top participants, the top regional outfitters working with the top gear manufacturers and other brands associated with a particular subculture. The reputation of place among the Obsessed draw the Interested to that place.

Figure 16: The business partnership in supporting a music event in Little River Blueway (photo by author)

Social Hint

The Capital Framework in a Destination Community

Dr. Cornelia Flora and Dr. Jan Flora, professors of Sociology at Iowa State University, specialized in the research of rural change and community development gave us a good overview of the spectrum of different types of capital involved in a community. In their Community Capital Framework, there are seven types of capital needed for a community to be vibrant, healthy and sustainable; particularly in the rural setting. These capital types are: natural, cultural, human, social, political, financial and built (see Figure 17). These seven areas are usually not static; they are capable of transforming into related forms of capital and always affect one another. In a tourism destination community, as presented in this book, all seven layers of capitals are planned and designed with careful and creative thoughts (see Table 1).

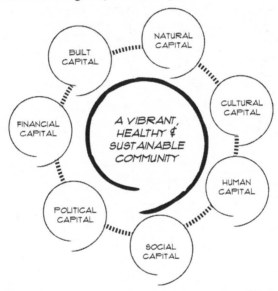

Figure 17: Seven types of capitals in the Community Capital Framework

Capital type	Community Framework Definition	Interpretation in the unique Destination Community characteristics
1. Natural Capital	Assets related to location, natural resources and the amenities based on the natural environment and beauty.	Amenities, natural resource based subcultures, etc.
2. Cultural Capital	How people "know the world" and their behaviors and communication based on their interpretation of the world. For example, languages, common beliefs and social values, rituals and customs, etc.	Learning about "who are our people" and "our tribes"; developing a compelling narrative of the community.

3. Human Capital	People's skills and abilities, as well as their ability to understand the body of knowledge and practice to achieve optimum outcome. For example, people's education, skills, health, creativity, youth, etc.	The "obsessed and interested;" the experts, team members, and business partners, etc.
4. Social Capital	The human connection and bonding between people and social groups. For example, trust, norms of reciprocity, network structure, cooperation, common vision and goals, leadership, depersonalization of politics, acceptance of alternative views, diverse representation, etc.	Sense of community, business partnership, the bonding experience within subcultures, the sharing experience between different subcultures, provide service to users, supportive business environment, etc. This is the "software" of the destination community.
5. Political Capital	The administration and political power to influence the rules and regulations, as well as the enforcement.	Becoming creative and "break" jurisdiction boundaries when categorizing and utilizing regional assets
6. Financial Capital	The financial resource to facility community's maintenance and development, and the accumulation of wealth for future community growth.	Focusing on the region when utilizing the assets, providing a supportive business environment, especially to the startup enterprises
7. Built Capital	The infrastructure that supports the community's functions. Such as telecommunication facilities, roads and main streets, housing, water and sewer system.	Maintaining the "hardware", the physical infrastructure, of the community

Table 1: The interpretation and application of seven types of capitals in a Destination Community

Human capital, among all the types, is one that usually is overlooked in community building. For a destination community that is built upon complementary subcultures, human capital is the key to success. Comparing to communities that have a civic or community center, where residents can practice their hobbies at the level of amateur, the emphasis on the dedication to the subcultures in the destination communities brings this passion for life to a higher level.

The "obsessed" see their passion as an art, and as they immerse themselves in the utmost enjoyable and extremely focused "flow" experience. Free from self-consciousness and time-awareness, their skills are improved. People are naturally drawn to the dedicated and skillful experts; in this sense, the "obsessed" are extremely valuable to the destination community. The "obsessed" attracts the "interested"; they together make the experience enjoyable for the "random", who will be likely to spread the good words after they leave. This is why understanding the importance of human capital in the destination community is crucial.

Another aspect of human capital is the employees in the community: people who work in the community. These people directly or indirectly provide services to the customers or contribute to the overall community development or policymaking. The human capital of the community staff, i.e. the level of professional, dedication, skills, education and passion, directly affects the efficiency, accuracy, effectiveness and creativity of their job performance.

Just like the "obsessed" is valuable in the user's group, it is advisable to recruit those who have a passion for their work and tend to experience "flow" during their job performance into our team. When the employees experience "flow" at work, they tend to perform their job at a higher energy level, are more creative, and present a more optimistic attitude. Optimism, for example, will likely increase the quality of service we provide to our users. A positive outcome of this is when a friendly, authentic and enthusiastic host-customer relationship is formed. Social capital and financial capital is collected for the destination community.

—

Chapter Summary

- There is no mass market. No interest majority. No way to get in front of the majority.
- Generic is dead. Compromising to the least offensive denominator is dead in destination communities.
- Handmade Tourism is a people business.
- For each subculture the Obsessed are your key human capital, both your ambassadors and your primary target market. They set the tone for the destination

community.

- Creating a destination culture allowing for participation beyond the Obsessed is key in attracting the Interested to a successful destination community.
- If you are remarkable, these people will tell others.
- We must embrace inter-related layers of complementary subcultures sharing the same natural resource.
- Your subcultures will drive your types of events and programs.
- The strong reputation of your place among the Obsessed will draw the Interested to you.

Chapter 4

BUILDING CONTEXT: DESIGNING AN INTERGRATED TOURISM SYSTEM

Integrated Tourism System design is an important strategy in building a destination community. As discussed in the previous chapter, the supporting pillars for a destination community are the complementary subcultures developed based on local resources and cultural atmosphere. The tourism assets of a community often seem to be self-evident to the local; however, they can often be lost from the visitors' point of view. It is actually quite difficult to relinquish ones point of view for another but it is necessary or the full story simply is not told in an understandable manner to the potential visitor.

The tourism destination system begins with an integrating mindset, cataloging all the tourism assets in your area, regardless of the boundaries between jurisdiction responsibilities. The system must allow the visitors to fully understand both how to enjoy all regional facilities and how to meet other needs during the visit regardless whether or not these needs are met by your particular organization. Don't worry about jurisdiction; inventory all the regional assets and build a strong narrative about it, which shows a straightforward and complete scenario to your visitors on how to have a good time and an authentic fulfilling experience in your community. This is the process of designing your integrated tourism system. This process always keeps the visitors point of view as the central planning thread.

A destination community is a community that reaps significant economic development benefits from having a tourism system. I am only interested in destinations that remain livable and engaging to the full and part time residents as it matures. I have worked in both mountain and coastal areas. In both, the tourism draw typically comes from naturally occurring subcultures based on the natural and cultural resources authentic to the area. The question is: what kind of destination can you authentically be? Systems must remain authentic to the nature of the area while also keeping relevant with current recreation and sporting trends. This allows systems to develop that are unique to the resort, municipality, or region the system is being designed for.

Integrated Tourism Systems for destination communities focus on the authentic user experience as the primary planning thread. How the user perceives and understands the potential experience of the overall system is as important as in attracting visitors. The quality of the operations of individual assets and destination building is important in delivering a quality experience building an authentic destination. These systems can be macro systems covering a region, or micro systems covering a single resort and their allied support services. The resulting destination must strive to deliver a triple bottom line: Economics – Conservation –Quality of Life.

Breaking the Jurisdiction Boundary

What are your tourism assets? From the visitors' point of view, it is all the authentic experiences and support available within the identifiable destination area. It is not all the assets owned by your particular agency or business. It is everything that is available to the visitor while he or she is in your area regardless of jurisdiction, ownership or affiliation. Jurisdiction lines are the often most fragmenting factor to the end user trying to understand the area (see Figure 18).

We are seeking to build an understandable narrative that a potential visitor will identify with on how they will use your area. People visit places: they are not solely coming to visit any one particular attraction, and their experience does not stop at the boundaries of our facility. The system must allow the visitor to understand both how to enjoy your facilities and how to meet the other needs during the visit regardless to weather those needs are met by your particular organization.

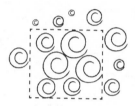

**BREAKING THE JURISDICTION BOUNDARY:
COLLECT ALL THE TOURISM ASSETS IN YOUR AREA**

Figure 18: Users at a destination community have the opportunity to enjoy all the assets of the place

Cataloging Tourism Assets

We focus on our visitors' experience. That experience does not stop at the boundaries of our facilities. When looking at your assets from an end user point of view, you begin to see existing and potential usage pattern. Why does something become a pattern? Patterns are created when combinations of activities are understandable and have a somewhat predictable outcome.

A pattern is a framework on which many variations can be hung but each with a recognizable outcome, which is often studied in order to search for the causal factors. In developing tourism systems, you are essentially creating systems and anticipating the major patterns that will result. Creating conditions for a tourist destination community is an art. It is not simply following a proven business plan and replicating a franchise. It is searching for the authentic experience contained with a region the way a sculptor searches for the shape that in authentically contained within the stone. It does not really matter what types of values your particular destination is based on as long as it is sincere to you and your target market.

Cataloging your tourism assets happens after you have integrated all the resources in your area, regardless of their jurisdiction and administration responsibilities. This is when you sort out and categorize the resources, for your own asset inventory. For the end users, each tourism visit has to have several different distinct needs met in order to be called a rounded experience. Each of these has opportunities for economic development but they also have commonalities relating them into a marketing unit. The primary needs consist of (also see Figure 19):

- Core Activities
- Lodging
- Dining
- Provisions
- Ancillary Activities –Recreation, Culture, Arts, Retail

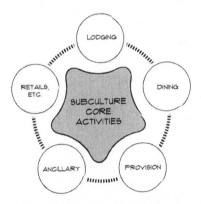

CATEGORIZING TOURISM ASSETS:
CORE ACTIVITIES AND FIVE TYPES OF SERVICES

Figure 19: The users at a destination community will be offered a rounded subcultural-entered experience

It is symbiotic relationships with other service providers. An asset business can fall anywhere within the core activities or within the secondary support services chain. As a tourism system matures, there may be many variations in quality, price point, and expectation levels for these needs, but each of them supports the core activities, not exclusively.

During the 2008 real estate crash I was working on a project on the GA / SC border. My project was to take a large formula style recreation based community, Savannah Lakes Village, and give it context and create a tourism based relocation destination. In other words, reposition it as a Destination Community. Two key elements many formula communities were left to deal with were context and an authentic identity. As a student in the late 80's, I had the opportunity to be on a task force with Hugh Morton of Grandfather Mountain, NC. He showed me the basics of building context.

The attractions of northwestern NC are not concentrated due to the geographic nature of the area. A key in developing the North Carolina High Country brand was looking at the comfortable range a visitor would travel within the region and creating an understandable narrative so the visitor can quickly understand how to use an area. Working separately, little towns like Valle Crucis, Aho, Foscoe, Linville, and Newland could have had the best individual stories and collateral possible and reached no where near the success level they did by falling under the context of a single regional brand.

For Savannah Lakes Village, (along with Kirk Smith the current COO) I developed a context region called, The Little River Blueway. I want to use the Little Blueway Project as an example and look at the Blueway Area tourism asset cataloging (see Figure 20 ,Table 2 and Figure 21). The full project analysis report is included in Appendix I.

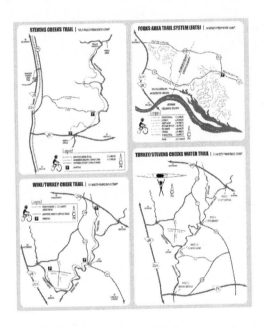

Figure 20: A graphic inventory of the trail assets in the Little River
Blueway Region (concept by David Twiggs and Kirk Smith)

	Catalog	Assets
Core Activities	**Land Based Trails**	1. Hickory Knob Hiking and Mtn. Biking Trails
		2. Baker Creek Hiking and Biking Trails
		3. Forest Service Roads
		4. Rails to Trails Program (currently in place)
	Land Based Organized Recreation Assets	1. Hickory Knob Golf Course – SC PRT*
		2. Tara Golf Course – SLV**
		3. Monticello Golf Course – SLV
		4. McCormick CC Golf Course – privately held
		5. Hickory Knob Skeet Range – SC PRT
	Existing Camping Assets	1. Baker Creek State Park – SC PRT
		2. Hickory Knob State Park – SC PRT
		3. Leroy's Ferry Campground – USACOE***
		4. Mt Carmel Campground – USACOE
		5. Hawe Creek Campground – USACOE
	Scenic and Historical Assets	1. Calhoun Mill Dam
		2. Badwell Cemetery, Home site and Springhouse
		3. Little River Quarry
		4. De La Howe Tomb
		5. Indian Massacre Grave Site
		6. Huguenot Worship Site
Lodging	**Existing Lodging Assets**	1. Hickory Knob State Park – SC PRT
		2. Savannah Lakes Resort and Conference Center – privately held
Dining	**Food and Beverage Assets**	1. Hickory Knob Lodge – SC PRT
		2. Monticello Grill – SLV
		3. Tara Clubhouse – SLV
Provision & Ancillary activities	**Motorboat Support Assets**	1. Village Store – Fuel and Groceries
		2. Savannah Lakes Marina – Fuel, Boat Rental and Supplies
		3. Hickory Knob – Canoe Rental
		4. Rays – Fuel and Groceries
	Fishing Tournament Facility	1. Dorn Fishing Facility – McCormick County
	Other Assets	1. Old 378 Visitor Center Building (Presently Unused)
		2. Quail Woods De La Howe Youth Camp
		3. De La Howe State School Wilderness Program
		4. De La Howe Barn and Interpretive Trail
		5. Savannah Lakes Medical Center

* SCPRT- SC Parks, Recreation and Tourism

** SLV - Savannah Lakes Village

*** USACOE – US Army Corps of Engineers

Table 2: *Tourism Asset Cataloging in Little River Blueway Area*

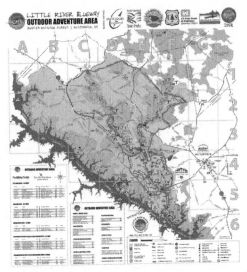

*Figure 21: An outdoor adventure map as part of the tourism informa-
tion package for Little River Blueway area (concept by David Twiggs
and Kirk Smith)*

Developing Compelling Narratives

You have cataloged your assets. You understand their opportunities and limitations in providing an authentic experience.
You must now build a compelling narrative to set an accurate
yet alluring expectation of investing time and resources into the
area as a visitor: the story of how to enjoy your area. The narrative, through various types of media, such as informative maps,
signs and collateral materials, creates communication and as-
surance for the visitors. Remember that your narrative and asset
catalog is also a key tool is attracting other tourism assets to
your system. People rarely invest when they cannot understand
how they will fall into the narrative of the system.

Too many potential destinations rely on what I call the rack
card approach to system development. They simply line up all
possible choices for the potential visitor to choose from (Figure
22). Typically these are organized by service categories, such as

Lodging, Dining, or Attractions.

There have been several studies showing that too many choices cause stress to the consumer. While those studies tend to focus on products, I believe it can be extrapolated to making experiential decisions. The rack card model simply shows a myriad of choices. It does not give the potential visitors a clear communication of their potential experiences based on their self-selected subcultures.

Figure 22: *The card rack model only provides its users with options, without "story" of the place (photo by author)*

People want to be with their "tribe," the subculture with whom they identify. A hand full of rack cards leaves the potential visitor with choices but no narrative. Members of a subculture tend to have similar preferences in lodging, dining, and entertainment but primarily they want to be around others in their subculture. Put together narratives focusing on each of your authentic and potential subcultures. Make each subculture understand their potential experience. Based on that anticipated experience, they will come. If the experience from that initial visit is authentic and satisfying, they will expand their exploration to additional visits and long term potential in migration. They will spread your story for you.

Each destination community normally ends up with several subcultures sharing some resources, individuals with interest in multiple subcultures, or other type of interrelationship (see Figure 23).

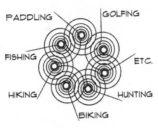

BUILDING AN INTEGRATED SYSTEM:
BASE ON COMPLEMENTARY SUBCULTURALS WITH
OVERLAPPING USAGE OF RESOURCES

Figure 23: The process of designing a Tourism Integrated System

Let me unpack the subculture mindset a bit. The reasons that building a compelling and complete narrative is extremely important are two fold. On one hand, users highly prefer to be able to predict the experience of their visit. Without the information provided for the potential users to analyze their experience in relation to their own particular user group, in terms of the suitability for specific ages and abilities, the users will find another location that they do understand through the available information on a destination community.

On the other hand, even when you think your part of the story is being told well (rack card approach,) but the users cannot easily understand how to create their entire experience (core activities, lodging, dining, provisions and recreation), they will, again, choose an area that can help them envision their whole trip. The pre-experience understanding gives the users the confidence to try the unknown. In the example of Little River Blueway project, the map (see Figure 24) shows not only the route and length of the trails, but also indicates the locations of other support services: lodging, dining, provision, and various kinds of recreation.

This map uses interesting illustration and perspective from the users' point of view; providing greater understanding of the potential experience. If the individuals are part of our targeted subculture, they are very likely the people who will be attracted if they get the feeling that the experience suits what they are looking for.

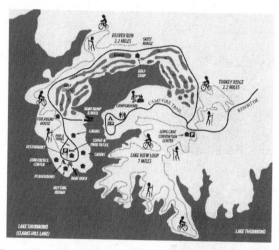

Figure 24: A complete, informative and visually interesting map shows the potential trail using experience in the Little River Blueway area (concept by David Twiggs and Kirk Smith)

Therefore, the readiness, easy-to-understand and completeness of the information about the destination are very important, when it comes down to attracting visitors and winning their choice over other destination systems. Through doing this, you let the visitors spend more time in your recreation destination, which results in higher visitor satisfaction, increased room nights and facility volume. Take the initiative and responsibility, and do not rely on other agencies to tell your story.

Bringing it to another Scale

One of my motivations for designing a model for an integrated tourism destination system is the need for this concept to be scalable. I am now applying the model to a region in central Arkansas, which I am calling the Ouachita High Country. The project is designed to build regional context for both the City Of Hot Springs and Hot Springs Village. Hot Springs Village is the 26,000-acre private community that has engaged me to move the project from a formula style community model to a tourism destination community. This project covers about 2.5 million acres and like the Little River Blueway, it focuses on the end user understanding how to use the region for an extended tourism visit (see Figure 25).

In our initial roll out to the Arkansas Department of Tourism, they encouraged us to expand the project area to include an additional million acres to the west. We chose to focus on our original target area but have plans to eventually expand to cover their recommendation.

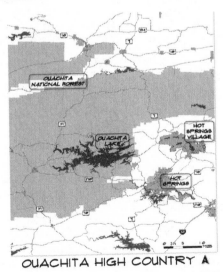

OUACHITA HIGH COUNTRY A

Figure 25: Ouachita High Country Region

Although a bigger project, Ouachita High Country is still comprised of day trip opportunities ranging from the Malvern Whitewater Paddling Park in the SE of the project area to Mt. Magazine State Park and Lodge, the highest peak in Arkansas, which anchors the NE corner. This allows a travel time maximum radius of about 2 hours from the primary lodging concentrations. That is a large range but feasible for extended stay, second homeowners and permanent in-migrating populations. Remember they moved here for the regional subcultures also.

Like the Little River Blueway, this project will create the region's outdoor recreation tourism information website but also be promoted through a quarterly lifestyle magazine distributed through all the primary towns, parks, and tourism centers in the region. Again, improving the tourist experience and opportunities will translate in additional room nights, restaurant covers and dollars spent in shops, stores and services in the region.

Because of the 2.5 million acre scope of the Ouachita High Country Project, we decided to start with creating the communications elements rather than the mapping elements as in the Little River Blueway Project. We developed a start up project of a lifestyle magazine aptly named *Ouachita High Country* to have a 40,000-copy distribution on a quarterly basis both within the region and all state welcome centers (see Figure 26). This allowed us to create dynamic content which we also leveraged into our OHC website www.ouachitahighcountry.com and Facebook presence (see Figure 27 and 28). With a steady source of engaging content, we also leveraged other social media platforms such as Twitter (see Figure 29).

The cataloging of the area is obviously much more extensive. Because of serving a bigger market I find it much easier to find substantial subculture partners.

Figure 26: *Cover of Fall 2014 Issue of Ouachita High Country Magazine*

Figure 27: *Screenshot of Ouachita High Country official website at http://ouachitahighcountry.com*

Figure 28: *Screenshot of Ouachita High Country Magazine Facebook page*

Figure 29: *Screenshot of Ouachita High Country Magazine Twitter feed "@OHCMagazine"*

This project is giving context for the region, but specifically for the project I am currently charged with, repositioning the 26,000 acre Hot Springs Village from the prerecession formula private community model into a multi faceted tourism driven destination community.

Hot Springs Village had no specific context nor did the region. Now the marketing of Hot Springs Village, Hot Springs, and any of the towns within the Ouachita High Country region have a greater context that greatly expands the messaging of authentic lifestyle choices available to market for tourism and relocation.

I often say that moving to Hot Springs Village (Hot Springs or any other place for that matter) does not consist of what is provided to you by a Property Owners Association, a city government, or a county. Moving to a place of quality consists of all the lifestyle and experience options provided to you by your region, be they public or privately owned.

Not only does this type of project give your destination context, it also gives a platform for "third party" validation of your advertisements and focus editorials alongside the grass roots project articles. Building a tourism destination system is basically a grass roots project. It is the provider communicating with the users. It takes some sophistication to take this grass root element and nuance it into an economic driver for the region, but done well it is very beneficial for all.

Bringing in elements such as appropriate residential and commercial real estate development takes conscious planning and discipline. The feel of this process is very grass roots. It is a cooperative effort between primarily the business entities, but also includes the governmental entities. Your partners will use the brand. Those you would rather not have using the brand will use it as well.

There are nuanced ways to protect the brand but remember you are naming a place, albeit a big one. You are not successful if the name is not spread. I don't worry about this much.

—

Social Hint

Why does an integrated tourism system work for a destination community?

The integrated tourism system for destination community, although it is a business model, it is also a social-symbiotic system. It incorporates in the function-oriented structure, assigning a position for each one: businesses, the business host and the users (see Figure 30). In every social structure, though, there are both functional and conflict aspects co-existing.

Comparing to the traditional "card rack" approach, the function aspect is promoted with a clear guideline, and the conflict comes from constructive competition, based on the quality of the business service and if any party fits into the development theme of the destination community.

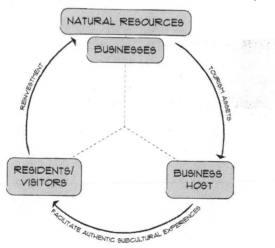

Figure 30: *The socio-symbiotic system between the parties in a tourism integrated system*

"Destination" implies a goal, a theme, a direction, and something different from a normal community. Let's look at "theme." Although it sounds exclusive, the wisdom in developing coexisting themes in a destination community is that it is based on promoting diversity and authentic experience through its subcultures that are suitable to the local resources. People come and enjoy their subcultures. When the system of subcultures is strong, it bonds people together, and people adopt the symbolic meaning from their experiences. This is when a subculture truly becomes a collective culture, where people feel belonging. With shared resources (see Figure 23), people from various subcultures have the opportunity to come together and socialize. Therefore, a sense of community is formed.

Jane Jacobs observes and claims that there are two driving forces in developing local economy, according to her book the *Economy of Cities*. The first is diversity, the second is import replacement. Diversity in the types and sizes of local businesses help a local economy to sustain; even when one business goes out, other industries and businesses will still be in place to hold up the local economy. Import replacement suggests that a community or a city replaces what used to be imported from other places with local products, in other words, to become self-sufficient or even export to other places.

In the integrated tourism system, there are several categories of diversity. The first is various parties in the partnership – local businesses, government entities, private resort communities, private parties, and the customers. Everybody is invited and once they are in, they function together in organic solidarity. Within each party, there are also diverse ingredients. For example, it welcomes local businesses, either long established or simply a startup. It also welcomes customers with different interests and lifestyles, which come for different complimentary subcultures. This diversity largely insures the resilience of economic breakdown. By cataloging its local assets into the five types; core activities, lodging, dining, ancillary, and provisions, it prepares tourism destination to be self-sufficient. When the visitors come and have a great time, they leave and spread the good words of the destination community. This is when resource export takes place.

—

Chapter Summary

- Designing an integrated tourism system always keeps the visitors point of view as the central planning thread.
- Systems must remain authentic to the nature of the area while also keeping relevant with current recreation and sporting trends.
- Systems are designed to develop uniquely for each individual resort, municipality, or region.
- How the user perceives and understands the potential experience of the overall system is as important as in attracting visitors.
- People visit places: they are rarely coming to visit any one particular attraction, and their experience does not stop at the boundaries of a facility.
- Brand beyond your borders! Catalog all assets in the logical visitor range while in your area.
- Build a compelling narrative to set an accurate yet alluring expectation of investing time and resources into the area as a visitor: the story of how to enjoy your area.
- Build narratives for each subculture you seek to attract based on their preferences.
- Members of a subculture tend to have similar pref-

erences in lodging, dining, and entertainment but primarily they want to be around others in their subculture.

- Visiting or moving to a place of quality consists of all the lifestyle and experience options available to you in your region, be they public or privately owned.
- Businesses don't invest until they understand how they will fall into the narrative of the system.

Chapter 5

THE BUSINESS MODEL FOR DESTINATION COMMUNITY: INTEGRATED TOURISM SYSTEM

In the Cataloging process discussed earlier, we saw how all types of people and small businesses can be tourism assets. These are often just subculture skills based in our resident obsessed practitioners, which are not a business as of yet. The process may also identify needs or assets you don't have in order to grow a particular subculture. A key to building a sustainable tourism economy base is creating an atmosphere of fostering and incubating businesses, especially small businesses. How do we create that atmosphere? If a subculture is authentic to your area, there are often individuals that would love to start a business or existing businesses that would love to expand into your area. We need to remember that most tourism businesses are market followers not market builders. We need to be the market builder.

In building destination communities we are market builders and identifying authentic experiences for visitation creates many opportunities for small businesses. Many tourism startups are personality driven. You will have a charismatic obsessed practitioner of a subculture working at a "day job." They are independent and often do not have the resources to simply start on their own. Jane Jacobs, one of the foundations of community building and urban planning once said in *The Death and Life of Great American Cities,* "new ideas must use old buildings." The relatively cheap rent on storefronts, warehousing and the like allows these lean startup organizations to get a foothold. However, in many outdoor-based startup businesses, a key stopping block can be finding locations to operate from or may be as simple as having someone to answer the telephone and make a reservation.

If we call the physical infrastructure the "hardware", I would like to offer alternative thinking on how we use another type of our existing infrastructures – the software. These are typically our business structures and partnerships. As we build our tourism system we are more concerned with creating to complete visitor/subculture system than we are with who "owns' a particular service. In other words we court, foster, and incubate the skills and services we need to complete a subculture experience narrative.

Who can incubate these businesses? Any existing organization with a complimentary mission should look at expanding their market by incubating these businesses. I have worked with the traditional partners such as Chambers, Visitor Bureaus, and government tourism agencies but have primarily found non-traditional partners such as large amenity based private communities, hotels and existing tourism businesses to be the best partners because they see a direct return. In all cases the mindset must be to treat the start up as an asset for the incubating partner. I have used the same systems for calling in tee times for my golf courses to make sporting guide reservations, spa appointments, or kayak rentals. All this expanded the offerings and opportunities for other outdoor activities to be scheduled through the same staff without increasing my costs. The same has been done through hotel staffs giving them an obvious marketing advantage over lodging only operations. As I often work with private resort communities, these additional services give my communities additional lifestyle subcultures to offer which opens them to a wider in-migration market and higher real estate sales and values.

Incubating Tourism Businesses

In developing tourism business assets, most areas will focus on growing locally based startups and attracting satellite operations from existing small and midsized businesses. To do this we build a due diligence package just as in any business recruitment activity except with a twist. We find sponsors and partnerships to facilitate these businesses.

For startups, things are often feasible on a micro scale that would not be feasible if courting a larger scale chain. For this we need to go beyond the old style Chamber of Commerce model (Old Chamber Model) in which a mature business joins a generalized host organization for a fee. The host organization acts as a clearinghouse for member information but rarely delivering an experience driven visitor focused narrative. One shortcoming of this model is that the hosting organizations thrive on long established existing members that can be resistant to any change. These organizations typically paint an area's story only in the broadest generic strokes in order not to offend any established members or alienate potential members. Also, because this is a membership fee based model, any business that is not a member of the organization will not be mentioned. In a community where tourism has not been an established part of the economic system, it can be seen as unimportant by some established businesses.

In an Old Chamber Model, the Chamber or its equivalent has staff on the payroll to answer calls and questions but often acts as a directory service only. "If you ask for a specific member business type we will look it up and answer you." It has the website but it is generalized to include all member businesses. In the traditional chamber model, someone who is visiting the area calls to find out the opportunities for finding a fishing guide. If the guide is a member of the chamber, the caller may be given the number to the guide. In the much higher likelihood that a startup is not a member of the chamber, the caller can often be told there are no businesses like that with the chamber – end of conversation and the visitor takes their money elsewhere.

In a supportive atmosphere, there should be the opportunity for lean startup with a much lower barrier for entry in tourism than other traditional industries. A lean startup is the starting of a business of little resources relying primarily on the talents of the entrepreneur. Because tourism is experiential at core, it is easier for talent to create small business to be directly paid by adding value to the experience. However, in an unsupportive environment many small towns and communities have experienced "Brain Drain" or "Youth Drain". It is when the young people in a community, after being educated, leave the area in search of satisfying opportunities and quality of life.

Take Dover as an example, a start-up fishing guide trying to use the unsupported model. Dover is a passionate and talented individual who has spent years learning the local waters and would love nothing more than to guide visitors on fishing trips of the area. Dover has the equipment to outfit the guests because of the ongoing personal passion for the activity. He is one of the Obsessed. On startup, however, Dover cannot simply quit his primary job and devote himself totally to building a clientele. Initially he must find a conductive location to meet the day's guests. Typically this is simply a boat ramp because he has no partnerships in place. When he is guiding he is out of touch. He focuses on providing good customer experiences and will not be detracted from it by answering cell phone calls to book future trips. If he does so, the client he is serving and the one on the phone with will each have a diminished experience, which makes them less likely to be return customers. He cannot adequately do both things at one time. He doesn't have the funds to join a chamber type organization nor were there adequate support structures in place for any perceived value to motivate joining. Diminished user experiences and customer service add up to fewer customers and less likelihood of building successful growing tourism business.

The Incubator Model For Integrated Tourism System

Now let's look at an incubator model for this same service. An established organization takes the role of tourism concierge for tourism businesses in the area. This organization may be the local chamber, a community association, visitor's bureau, a non-profit, a lodging vender, or any other organization whose purpose or business model could benefit from tourism. Regardless, the organization has made the decision that growing these startup businesses is important to the economic development and livability of the area. In this case, a private resort community wants to focus the entire area as a regional destination not only to enhance the quality of life and the livability of the area, but also to build return on investment through the marketability of homes and condos within the master-planned area to a new target market. The community already has staff to answer the phones and the website to market the area. They are already offering other services such as restaurant and golf. In the end, it is vital for a handmade tourism destination to establish an entrepreneurial outlook on how these independent interests tie together in the eyes of the end user.

Back to Dover's case, seeing the potential of the fishing resources as a motivation to visit and move to the area, the organization actively sought out Dover through asking around for good fishing guides in the area. An opportunity was presented to Dover in which Dover would be featured as Head guide for the community on a new page within the existing community website focusing on the fishing opportunities. The standardized price list and trip description was developed so the expectations of experience could accurately be set by the existing telephone and reservation staff. The trips for Dover's clients were booked in much the same way the community was reserving tee times or dinner reservations. There was even a deposit system created so that Dover would be somewhat protected from clients not showing up.

Dover remained independent and the community advertised his services as part of the lifestyle offered to the visitor or resident. As the program became more popular over time, Dover saw the opportunity to start a small shop and organize other guides. He not only continued partnering with the community, but also the hotels and restaurants. As Dover's business continued to grow, the community that incubated Dover's business in the early stages no longer actively incubates the business; but to benefit from the lifestyle and marketing returns from having the new business adding to the tourism culture of the region.

Tourism Destination System And Entrepreneurial Partnership

A key to designing a tourism system is to identify which subcultures your different assets can support and work your design to them. Assets are often human capital. We can help bring these fledgling high knowledge / high touch businesses along. We should also look at our existing business and see how they can be incorporated.

Outdoor recreation is typically organized through a subculture. Let's use mountain biking as an example. Your facility, Riverside Campground, has a great 3 mile single track trail built to be an amenity to your camping areas. In the ordinary system, your marketing point is likely to be "come camp out and bike our trails." In most cases this is as far as the efforts go. This may result in some overnights, many more day uses on the trail, and minor revenue impact. You get relatively minor benefits in terms of camp nights if the other elements of the tourism synergy are not in place.

In building a destination system, the scenario would be completely different. *Handmade tourism is entrepreneurial in nature.* We look at all the possible experiences the user could have while staying at but not exclusively on your facility. To design your destination system, you need to start with cataloging all the tourism assets in your area. When this is done, you end up with this inventory (see Table 3):

ASSETS	NOTES
Salem's BBQ	3 miles outside of your gate
Dover Fishing Guide Service	4 Miles
A USFS 6 Mile Single Track	15 Miles
A State Park with 8 miles of single track	18 Miles
Off the Chain Bike Shop	35 Miles

Table 3: Asset inventory example

Looking at these assets, we begin with building partnerships. Meet with the owner of the BBQ and arranged for a 10% discount for Campers in appreciation for advertising the BBQ on your website "Salem's BBQ: the Official BBQ of Riverside Campground and Mountain Bike Races." Mountain Bike Races, you ask? Partnering with the Off the Chain Bike Shop in a regional city, a time trial race on the 2 Riverside Trails was developed and promoted as a regional event. The two trails were named/branded as the "Grinder" and the "Rock Sprint Loop." A thing of value should have a name. It helps in building both the marketing narrative and the user memories. The race was held and time trial results were kept for each race by class. These results were posted in the training section of your website so folks can ride against the winning times for practice. Specific warm up weekends can be marketed as pre jams.

In addition to your 3 miles of newly branded trails, Riverside Campground is now within 20 minutes of 14 miles of additional trails. These were "claimed" and marketed as additional places to ride, increasing the average stay by additional nights. You are the base for 17 miles of trail. In season you have worked a deal with a local band to play weekends at the BBQ and advertise meet ups with other riders for that post ride beer.

You have now partnered and cross marketed with two other businesses, "claimed" an additional 14 miles of single track for your patrons to ride during their stay, arranged for key night entertainment to entice additional overnights, and branded an event that gives training significance to your trails as well as exposure and recurring interest. The result is that by building a compelling narrative, your destination gets profit from higher visitor satisfaction, increased room nights and facility volume. That is why, from an entrepreneurial stand point, tourism has direct and positive benefits.

This is a much better story for the potential visitor to visualize. From a user point of view, you have created a subculture destination that brings the mountain biking "tribe" together for both sport and social experience. They can quickly make up a story in their head about what their trip will be like. It is an experience they can picture in their mind prior to coming. Fulfill that story and you are becoming a place of belonging with emotional attachments for the "tribe." The "tribe" then starts programming your facility for you. There are emotionally attached to the place. Now we determine which complimentary sub-cultures can also use the resources without diluting the experience.

As a regional tourism development entity, this simple but complete subculture narrative has become part of your integrated system experience inventory. You will build on this with other complimentary subcultures. As the area most likely has additional trails not open to biking, what about ultra trail runners or off road triathlons. Are there rivers suitable for paddling? What about a yoga gathering? Are there historical elements suitable for creating an auto trail? Is there golf? Not all subcultures must be similar to be complimentary to the same region.

The folks visiting the art shops and restaurants may have little in common with obsessed paddlers other than a general appreciation for the natural or cultural assets of the area but they can both be part of the system. My point is to seek other subcultures that appreciate your natural resources and start building a destination.

Creating a Team to Build An Integrated Tourism System

While learning our core passion activities may have taken us years of painstaking practice, study or research; the majority of the market is simply coming for an opportunity to belong and learn. To create the conditions for belonging, one simply has to put our passions authentically out there. Pick your point of view and that will determine your team. There is no need for college degrees, special certification course or credentialing to be passionate about the cultures within your area. Nor is there required experience level, just passion will do. Much great human capital is overlooked because of these arbitrary unnecessary standards. We need basic human interactions done well. No one is going to be passionate about creating an economic system for a destination community unless they love the area, feel the need for economic growth, and they have direct benefit from the results of the process.

If you have an area with true quality of place that has real potential to be an authentic destination community, how do you realize the economic development? You must start with putting together a team. It is important to keep the team as small and prioritized as possible. Only bring on passionate believers in the project, who are willing to put in the time in the short run. There will be many others along the process that will be lukewarm. They may be pro or con. They may or may not understand the potential benefits or detriments. They may only see the negatives or not see the potential negatives of uncontrolled unplanned growth. A good core team is required to overcome these impediments. In building your team for destination community, these are the elements that you need to consider (see Figure 31).

- Define business structure. Augment your recreation programs with complimentary outside programs. Build out the core activity, lodging, entertainment and provision matrix to identify smaller partners.
- Private entities & community associations. Go through the cataloging process to find the private entities that will most directly benefit from the area becoming more attractive to in-migration. Community associations are often major drivers that already have marketing budgets that are often being spent on much less attractive or ineffective ad campaigns.
- Private professional community. The private professional community often can easily donate in-kind work that is vital to the start up if they are aware of the need. Be strategic.
- Governmental partners. Look at necessary governmental partnerships. You may simply be putting feathers in their cap rather than receiving any tangible support at first. These are your partners and can be great in expediting the project; but raise your initial funding privately, if possible.
- Planning and policymaking. Find resources for land planning and development policy creation early in the process. Create value for underutilized public/civic spaces. Do project beyond your facility and focus on the big picture.

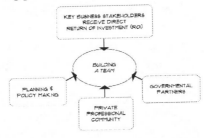

ELEMENTS TO CONSIDER WHEN BUILDING A TEAM

Figure 31: Elements to consider when building a team

Government facilities are often the least programmed areas of all venues. They were easy to fund and build but are often not programmed well. To avoid political stagnation, it may be preferable to legalize the team as an independent non-profit or simply a private entity.

—

Social Hint
"Friends" or "Enemies"

Building an integrated system in a tourism destination community, from a sociology point of view, is shifting the focus from the conflict oriented Old Chamber Model to the function and cooperation oriented incubator model.

In the sociology sense, conflict is not a bad term. It is a word for "competition" and "power struggle" for different groups. Many people, including sociologists, think this is the driving force for a society to move forward. However, when competition becomes the primary dynamic of a social structure, it may cause dysfunction in the social group. Just to be clear, any cooperation, political entity or business partnership is a social group, where people work on the same task together for common interests.

It is shown in Table 4 that in the Old Chamber Model, the businesses have to pay the entry fee to get on the directory of local business causes exclusivity from the business point of view, instead of thinking from the users' point of view. Conflict is induced from the very first step of the business partnership. Different from the Old Chamber Model model, the supportive incubator model does introduce conflict/competition too, but from the users' point of view. No matter if it is a fresh startup, or a long established business, everybody starts with the same support from the local business host, be it a Home Owners' Association, Chamber, or a grassroots nonprofit. Businesses, big and small, perform at different levels to serve the costumers. When the customers enter the picture, they function as the selectors according to their quality of service in the process of "evolution" of local business, if you will.

Dover's business is very likely to survive, if the call-in for reservation can be handled by the business host just like they handle other bigger business. In that way, all Dover needs to do is concentrate on delivering good service and building a personal bond with his customers.

	Old Chamber Model	Tourism Integrated System Incubator Model
Businesses	Bigger businesses tend to be supported, while smaller ones may be unsupported and excluded	All tourism asset businesses are encouraged, and passion for fitting in the narrative and provide good service is required
Business host	Non-selective/ Membership Based. Takes all businesses in.	Inviting, well structured, developing compelling narratives to support all asset businesses
Users/customers	Anyone with the fe to join.	Invited to become part only if it expands "story"
Economic development atmosphere	Overly competitive. Supportive but random	Supportive, inclusive, function-oriented, with a clear development theme

Table 4: The relationship between businesses, the business host and users/customers

The tourism integrated system incubator model focuses only on tourism asset businesses that add to the development of a destination community. It invites all tourism businesses, big and small, to get on board. It also requires the business host to be well organized and support the local business. In organizing the business host itself, it recruits like-minded team members, supportive business partners and other professional partners who agree on the economic development agenda for the local tourism.

The visitors and users ultimately become part of the

story, by participating and embracing, as well as becoming the local complementary subcultures at their choice. The integrated tourism system model truly promotes the functioning and cooperating aspects, rather than the conflicting, of the local economic atmosphere to a great degree.

—

Chapter Summary

- We need to be the market builder. Remember that most tourism businesses are market followers.
- We court, foster, and incubate the skills and services we need to complete a subculture experience narrative.
- Look for both traditional and non-traditional partners to incubate and foster new businesses
- Handmade tourism is entrepreneurial in nature.
- A thing of value should have a name. It helps in building both the marketing narrative and the user memories.
- Seek other subcultures that appreciate your natural or cultural resources and start building and incubating the businesses to become a destination.
- These additional services give communities additional lifestyle subcultures to offer which opens them to a wider in-migration market and higher real estate sales and values.

Chapter 6

THE GROWTH OF A DESTINATION COMMUNITY

We want to enhance our communities, not turn them into unlivable business zones. Typically it takes a lot of time and effort to create an integrated tourism system to serve a destination community. During this period, problems with growth can slip in gradually if not considered from the start. Great destination communities are great places. Great places to live, work, play and visit. This chapter will outline a few of the considerations that will help keep it a great place.

Conservation and Controlled Growth

It has been discussed earlier that, if we want to achieve sustainable and smart growth, we need to set a limit of development for our destination community. Most small communities do not need or want to attract millions of visitors per year. There are many ways growth can be controlled, but these are best determined prior to spurring the growth and putting appropriate checks and balances in place. One important development practice is the conservation communities. That is the development of large tracts of land with the concentrated high density residential surrounded by conserved but recreationally usable open space.

I recently had an opportunity to spend a couple of days touring the Santa Lucia Preserve to study their model as a conservation community. With 30,000 acres tucked in between the hills of Big Sur and Carmel by the Sea, California, Santa Lucia Preserve is an excellent example of conservation development to preserve a highly sensitive environment and the ranch culture of the 1800's.

Of Santa Lucia Preserve's 30,000 acres, approximately 28,000 acres are permanently preserved in conservation easements. The 300 homes spread through the property must be low impact, vernacular to the region, and not impact the view shed of the property. This is an ultra-high end development that was intentionally designed to save an extremely natural and culturally sensitive piece of private property.

All conservation communities need not be grand or exclusive. There are many opportunities for quality conservation projects on the edges of small, rural towns. The open space of a small farm can be preserved with greater housing density surrounding. The key is for the open space to be of value to the surrounding area, allowing the value to be relocated through additional entitlements in a flexible and innovative plan.

A failing example is the Sugar Top development on Sugar Mountain, NC. In the early 1980's the area was becoming established as a destination area through primarily local business investment. These local interests were sensitive to the environmental and social impact on the small town Appalachian culture. These were local developers with an innate desire to protect the region. They never envisioned any development that would harm the area and built no protections from it. As growth began to really spur, proper building controls were not in place to insure the continual existence the key elements of the local tourism advantages, for example, view shed.

The term "view shed" had probably not even been uttered in the area. It was simply assumed that no one would build anything that would detract from the area's beauty and livability.

As property values rose, making higher cost construction profitable, a group of real estate developers from a neighboring state began planning a 10 story high-rise condominium directly on top of one of the highest peaks in the region. At 5000 feet elevation with 180 degree unobstructed view, the developers boasted the finest view in the region. Unfortunately, it also put the structure as the preeminent feature on the skyline from all other mountains in the region and was able to be seen from many miles away. This prompted the local planning commission into action, but it did not happen in time to prevent the eyesore from impacting the view shed of hundreds of thousands of acres.

I include this worst case story to remind our growth policy makers, public or private, to not simply rely on antiquated Euclidian zoning models that make up many of our planning documents in rural areas. While most rural areas have for years believed that if they could simply push water and sewer lines further into the countryside, the development spurring with the tax windfall would fix all the illnesses of the budget. In fact the opposite is true.

Conservation community design and infill development practices are making tax-based growth much more sustainable without negatively impacting the natural features and open space. Because we are looking at conservation community practices on existing developed land, in order to concentrate densities and potentially decommissioning some elements of the infrastructure and to reduce the long term carrying cost of maintenance while increasing new unit yield. Randall Arendt has spoken and written extensively on this type of development. I believe the capital markets and consumer preferences are aligning and we will see more conservation community types in the future.

Controlling growth to shape outcomes in our community that we want to see is the most important element in destination community development. This is not about maximizing tax revenues, capital gains, or corporate profits at any cost. This is about making our communities the most enjoyable, sustainable and competitive places possible while maintaining good economic stability and fostering citizenship and stewardship.

A Mature Tourism System

A mature tourism system is one that has reached appropriate levels of growth and economic impact to satisfy the quality of life concerns with the sustainability factors of natural and social resources. A system can be overdeveloped and degraded without proper planning and controls. What is appropriate? It will differ from community to community. Some natural areas have reached maximum visitor tolerances before we see resource degradations. Other limitations are based on the impact on social resources such as traffic tolerance. When determining appropriate levels of community development, the planning of the growth quality is extremely important.

It should be remembered that relocation is often as big or bigger an economic driver for the region as visitation dollars. Relocation to a destination community is part of the normal progressions for visitors that have an emotional investment in the area. This is normally a combination of second home and retirement market. Both bring disposable income and lower need for government services. This must be included in the tourism plan.

There are several potential stages that a destination tourism system can experience (see Figure 32). Protecting your community from the negative latter stage consequences is vital to being a sustainable great place.

- Resource Potential – The authentic nature and physicality of a region will support certain recreational subcultures.
- Local Use / System Identification – Typically a region's potential will have been discovered by someone locally. These individuals understand how to use these resources for the particular recreational

activities.

- Symbiotic Local and Tourism Usage – A state of balance is reached when the local and tourism usage balance between economic growth and livability. This destination is now a great place to live and a great place to visit.

- Tourism Dominance Reduced Livability – An area left unchecked can become tourism usage dominant with livability becoming reduced. Typically as livability declines so will local control of tourism growth. Locally controlled tourism growth has a much less likelihood of over developing to its own detriment. Outside investment control can begin to dominate with profits a much higher priority than livability or sustainability.

- Tourism Overuse / Resource Degradation – Tourism usage becomes maximized for profits to the point that the tourism asset becomes degraded.

- Tourism Quality Declines – Tourism Asset value declines and does not attract the quality of tourist once attracted. Lowered revenues quickly are seen as declining maintenance in hospitality venues.

- Resource Collapse – Without recovery of the original resource potential the area will typically collapse with no remaining value as a tourism asset or as a quality place to live.

Figure 32: The stages of destination community may experience without controlled growth

It is obviously in our best interest to keep tourism growth in Symbiotic Local and Tourism Balance Stage. This keeps livability as a top priority and tourism in an economic development perspective to serve the locals rather than displace them. Development discipline must be put in place early with conservation goals so that the growth can be can be controlled early. Know when enough is enough. Don't be greedy.

—

Social Hint
More on the life cycle and sustainability of a destination community

Looking at the growth and life cycle of a community is about putting what we do in perspective. A community's growth and life cycle depends on, from users' point of view, the condition of its physical infrastructure, its functionality according to people's lifestyle, and the suitability of the ongoing societal value.

It is observed that the millennial generation weights experience more than ever. It is said in a Wall Street Journal interview that, the US society is moving to an "experience economy," where people invest in obtaining experiences more than possessing something. Destination communities must consider the consciousness towards such shift in the social values in America and even on the global realm to be socially successful. By developing complementary subcultures and providing people with authentic experiences, it meets all three criteria of a community for people to find fulfillment in all levels of human needs.

This is sustainable development in the social aspect (see Figure 33): people gravitate towards places that can meet their higher levels of human needs and care about their wellbeing in the long run. Sadly, many communities oftentimes overlook this, as these social needs are thought to be soft, abstract and hard to measure, as opposed to simply building another formula community, which has been proven financially successful elsewhere.

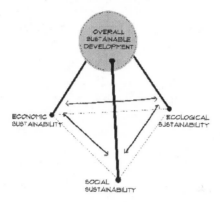

THE TRIPOD MODEL OF
SUSTAINABLE DEVELOPMENT

Figure 33: *The tripod model of sustainable development*

Access to nature, in many urban residential neighborhood-based communities, is not on the top of the list of concerns, other than people's plants and landscape in their yards. If we see a city or a metropolitan area as a mega community, then on edge of the community is nature. Conservation is critical from the economic and ecological sustainability point of view.

American cities that are on the cutting edge of smart growth such as Portland, Oregon and San Jose, California have been implementing "urban growth boundary" to restrain urban sprawling as the consequence of inefficient land-use and leapfrog-type development. The tourism destination communities in this book are mostly rural; nature and outdoor oriented communities. Therefore the relationship between the community and nature is even closer. From the social point of view, people move to these communities because they want to fulfill their passion for getting close to nature. From the ecologic point of view, the quality of the nature environment is immediately and directly related to the quality of life in the community. Finally, from economic point of view, the better natural environment, the more possibility for different subcultures to be developed with better quality in the community, and thus people will more likely to spend more time, come back to visit or relocate into the community.

In order to determine the suitability for developing a tourism destination community, inducing an existing one into another scale or introducing different subcultures requires us to study the site or community as each are unique and will react differently to the inputs. Tourism destination community is not a formula model, as many suburban neighborhoods with "cookie cutter" houses have been in the past. Authentic experience is one of the core values of tourism destination communities. Every natural site and cultural setting provides a different experience; it is up to us, the community developers to discover the potential of each place. One thing universal is, for a community to have a longer life cycle, we need to keep all three aspects of sustainability in mind.

—

Chapter Summary

- Just as people evolve to focus on human needs higher up Maslow's Hierarchy, our design of place both from the physical and psychological viewpoint must seek to serve the higher purposes.
- Growth problems can slip in gradually if not considered from the start.
- Conservation community development can be an

important tool as in-migration housing develops.

- Capital markets and consumer preferences are aligning and we will see more conservation community types in the future.
- A mature tourism system is one that has reached appropriate levels of growth and economic impact to satisfy the quality of life concerns with the sustainability factors of natural and social resources.
- Keep livability as a top priority and tourism in an economic development perspective to serve the locals rather than displace them.
- Development discipline must be put in place early with conservation goals so that the growth can be can be controlled early.
- Know when enough is enough. Don't be greedy.

Chapter 7

START BUILDING YOUR COMMUNITY

Bringing authentic tourism, vacation, and retirement relocation into your community, town, or region should always
be looked at as one of the tools for economic development and
smart growth. It may only be a part of the entire economic picture but someone must champion it for it to have impact. The
suitability and potential scale of your area will vary greatly with
other areas. None of this makes any significant difference. You
are what you are and there is someone out their interested in
that.

Handmade tourism communities organize existing assets and
find their target market. They create the conditions for attracting or starting the businesses needed to round out the experience. Revenues should be reinvested to enhance your region as
a unique destination and to have proper planning to be sure the
growth will be beneficial. All these things are part of the "to do"
list that comes only after we start. As this is a journey of dis-
covery about your community, the opportunities only become
evident as you explore. It is much more important to start than
to be ready.

Are you qualified?

If you are willing to reach out and open your passions to others you are qualified. You are not trying to draw everyone to
your destination. You want the ones that embrace your passions
and values; those that love your natural and cultural assets and

want to protect them. First, decide that you can do this. All great journeys begin with a step into the unknown.

"Who do you think you are to start this project?" I was asked this many times when I began naming regions, trails, and sections of rivers in my region. Who was I to tell this story? In my case, I run rural recreation based master planned communities that would be huge beneficiaries of becoming established as serious sporting destinations and places that subculture tribes were drawn. The small towns where I was located would equally benefit. I recognized this and saw that no one was taking up this torch. Everyone was busy looking at the world from his or her own business or agencies point of view; there was no cohesive story from the potential visitor point of view being told. I just decided to do it myself. I just started.

Some of my first partners were the recreation lodging and dining folks in the area because they could see the direct benefit. First, I looked at the government's regional plans for these rural areas, which are typically vague, but often mention outdoor recreation and tourism. Why do they mention tourism? It is hard for an agency to openly say we have no plan for you; you are in the middle of nowhere. You are not a great place for corporate headquarters, high tech R&D, or manufacturing. Because plans for the rural areas are difficult to make, the vague notion of tourism and outdoor recreation often makes it into the plan. So when I went to the government agencies, I thanked them for the idea and let them know that we we're moving ahead with their tourism plans and are not asking for any money. Putting feathers in people's caps get you much further than crying about what their reports say.

If they felt the region has other opportunities they would say so in the planning reports. If you agree, you should pursue those plans if you wish. I am in the traditional sporting, action sports, club sports, vacation and retirement real estate, and tourism businesses, so that is what I put my energies toward. The traditional economic development strategies are great and I support my region's efforts as long as they protect the natural resources of the area. I want to build destination communities and you probably do too if you have read this much of the book. By the way, great livable communities are becoming a big factor in attracting traditional business to an area. So becoming a great place raises all boats. Whoever has the vision has the qualification and can create the authority.

Back of the Napkin Startup

I view building a tourism destination system as bootstrapping a startup. The exciting part about this to me is that there are so few models to guide us. We can see areas of success and draw conclusions but there is no exact model for you to copy. I start by simply asking a few simple questions.

1. What Do People Enjoy Doing In Your Region?
2. What Are The Best Places In Your Region?
3. What Are All The Assets In Your Region?
4. Who Knows How These Assets Are Used?
5. Who Likes Using What?
6. Build The Narratives About How To Experience Your Assets.
7. What Missing Links Are In Your Narrative?
8. Who Would Benefit From Becoming A Great Destination?
9. What is Your Best Platform To Tell Your Stories?

From the first question, I let the answers evolve and expand. Each element becomes a different narrative on how a specific subculture will understand using the region. What your assets and needs are. Who will be your team. Build your stories and then set them free. Best Kept Secrets often fail.

While creating an integrated tourism system may sound technical and daunting, think of it as building a great place. Why do you want to visit there, work there, or live there? That is a story to tell. This process is creative and exciting. It adds to traditional economic development efforts. It is a path that will unwind as you follow it. All you have to do is start.

———

Chapter Summary

It is much more important to start than to be ready. Whoever has the vision has the qualification and can create the authority.

Ask a few simple questions.

1. What Do People Enjoy Doing In Your Region?
2. What Are The Best Places In Your Region?
3. What Are All The Assets In Your Region?
4. Who Knows How These Assets Are Used?
5. Who Likes Using What?
6. Build The Narratives About How To Experience Your Assets.
7. What Missing Links Are In Your Narrative?
8. Who Would Benefit From Becoming A Great Destination?
9. What is Your Best Platform To Tell Your Stories?

Just Start!!!!

LIST OF TABLES

—

LIST OF FIGURES

—

APPENDIX I

—

Overview Of Little River Blueway Project

In order to give the reader a context project overview on a scale that is more typical than my current 2.5 million acre project, I have included the initial project summary for the Little River Blueway Project in the Sumter National Forest of SC. Kirk Smith was instrumental of the layout of this report. As you will see in the report, we started with projects as a group of private sector businesses prior to seeking participation from SC Parks, Recreation and Tourism, the US Forest Service, and the US Core of Engineers. These groups saw that we had already committed our resources and were not asking for hard dollar funding, supported the project and allowed us much greater penetration into the region.

The Little River Blueway Project

In order to facilitate this and future projects, a 501(c)(3) non-profit has been created. This new organization is called Outdoor Initiative Inc. and is currently under review by the US Department of Revenue prior to approval. Document was finished on March 1, 2010.

PROPOSED PROJECT LOGO

—

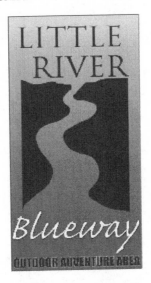

PROJECT LOCATION MAP

—

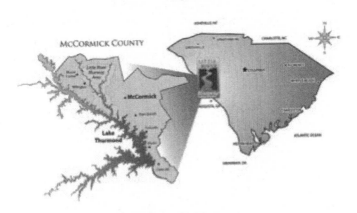

Project Summary

Based on the concepts outlined in the 2009 SC Tourism Plan for the region and the TIPS Strategies Economic Development Study for McCormick County SC, The Little River Blueway Project, has been planned to create a comprehensive outdoor recreation system. At the core of the project is a system of water and land based trails creating a "new" recreation system that can be a centralized platform from which to support and market other existing public and commercial recreational infrastructure.

The key opportunity is to centralize the marketing of all existing recreational assets that have been only sporadically marketed independently of each other. As established in the economic development studies listed above, tying all of our assets into an outdoor recreation system and using them to brand this region of McCormick County as a destination for these types of activities provides a much higher rate of return than trying to promote individual towns, facilities, and commercial entities.

Once the area is branded and draws new users from other markets, individual towns and entities have an established user base for business development projects and for building awareness of particular areas of commercial interest.

This system will allow user-friendly access to a variety of existing recreation infrastructure through consolidated information development, mapping, and marketing. This project area was determined by the availability of existing SC PRT, USACE, Forest Service and commercial recreational assets operating in the area.

These assets represent a significant preexisting capital investment with ample capacity to handle larger number of visitors. This project is intended to contribute to both the recreational and economic development goals of the two studies aforementioned.

Goals

- Develop the project area as a destination for water and land based outdoor recreation pursuits drawing users from South Carolina and Georgia statewide target markets.
- Define a marketable area of organized outdoor rec-

113

reation infrastructure to increase usage traffic to area towns and public facilities.

- Create opportunities for entrepreneurs and small business development within the northwestern McCormick County region.
- Generate usage at area parks, campgrounds, lodging, and commercial entities.
- Generate exposure and visitations to area municipalities and rural areas to create opportunities for economic development and job creation.
- Create scalable and ongoing programming to generate sustainable usage at parks, campgrounds, restaurants, lodging, and commercial entities.

Tactics

- Create and map a comprehensive inventory of existing recreational, natural, and historic assets.
- Develop appropriate marketing media and strategies to create awareness within defined target audiences
- Develop and grow recurring outdoor recreation sporting events.
- Develop additional key recreational assets to allow greater access and usage.
- Show interconnectivity of recreational assets owned by various public and private entities through mapping and collateral marketing materials.
- Organize infrastructure into system that supports varied cultural and educational programming.

Plan Elements

- Water Based Trail System
- Consolidate Hiking and Mountain Bike Trail Mapping

- Scenic Route with Natural and Historical Interpretive Materials
- Ongoing Recreational and Cultural Programming

I.
Water Based Trail System

According to the National Sporting Goods Association, paddling sports now have a user base of over 8 million active participants in the US and is experiencing continued growth. Several factors have contributed to the growth of paddling. Paddling fits well into the trend for greener, simpler, and more physically active lifestyles. Kayak design has evolved and offers comfort, stability, and ease of use. Affordable models are readily available to the beginner and novice market. Paddling has a wide user base demographic and is suitable for family activities with relative few participants interested in extreme type paddling. Most participants focus their destinations on calm waters that are appropriate for novice skill levels. Touring and fishing have become primary kayak activities. This element is designed to develop a series of river trails along the Little River and Long Cane Creek in McCormick County, SC.

See proposed project map below (Proposed Accesses Marked with "P" on Red Block)

ROUTES AND SECTIONS ANALYSIS:
—

This element proposes three primary water trail routes, each incorporating both natural and historical elements as points of interest. An additional southern route is included as primarily a motorboat route into the Baker Creek Pavilion Area. With all access points operational there would be approximately 37 miles of diversified water trails. These routes will provide a variety of paddling experiences all based in a concentrated geographic area terminating in a hub of existing SC State Park, USACE,

Forest Service and commercial recreational infrastructure.

PRIMARY ROUTES:
—

- ## Little River Route:

Sections	Put-In	Rest Area / Take-out	Length in Miles
Calhoun Mill	Calhoun Mill Steel Bridge	Mars Bridge	2.5
Mt Carmel	Mars Bridge	Morrah Bridge Backwaters	4
Willington	Morrah Bridge	Backwaters Little River Quarry Bridge	2.5
Bordeaux	Little River Quarry Bridge	Lone Cane Creek Boat Ramp	3
Huguenot	Lone Cane Creek Boat Ramp	Huguenot Worship Site	0.5
Pettigrew	Cut Huguenot Worship Site	Buffalo Creek Ramp	2.75
Baker Creek	Buffalo Creek Ramp	Baker Creek Boat Ramp	1.1
		Total	16.35

- ## Long Cane Route:

Sections	Put-In	Rest Area / Take-out	Length in Miles
Cherokee	Bradley Bridge (Long Cane Rd)	Patterson Bridge (Charleston Rd)	1.46
Indian Massacre	Patterson Bridge (Charleston Rd)	Hwy 28 Boat Ramp	4.6
De La Howe	28 Bridge Boat Ramp	Lone Cane Creek Boat Ramp	2.1
Huguenot	Lone Cane Creek Boat Ramp	Huguenot Worship Site	0.5
Pettigrew	Cut Huguenot Worship Site	Buffalo Creek Ramp	2.75
Baker Creek	Buffalo Creek Ramp	Baker Creek Boat Ramp	1.1
		Total	12.51

- ## Buffalo Creek Route

Sections	Put-In	Rest Area / Take-out	Length in Miles
Buffalo Creek	Badwell Cemetery	Buffalo Creek Ramp	2.2
Baker Creek	Buffalo Creek Ramp	Baker Creek Boat Ramp	1.1
		Total	3.3

- ## Optional Termination Point 378 Bridge Ramp

Sections	Put-In	Rest Area / Take-out	Length in Miles
Pavilion Cove	Baker Creek Boat Ramp	378 Bridge Ramp	1

All routes presently terminate at Baker Creek State Park Ramp. There is an optional termination take out at the 378 Bridge Ramp for paddlers staying in other camping areas. This option will add .3 miles to the overall length of all routes.

The Dorn Route is an open water route tying the Hawe Creek Camping Area and Dorn Fishing Facility to the Baker Creek Pavilion Cove. This route is not anticipated to be a primary canoeing route due to it going into the open waters of Lake Thurmond. It is important to include on the map to show an alternative ramp for motorboats and showing connectivity between the Hawe Creek Campground and the Baker Creek Pavilion Cove area.

- Dorn Route

Sections	Put-In	Rest Area / Take-out	Length in Miles
Hawe Creek	Hawe Creek Boat Ramp	Dorn Fishing Facility	0.6
Dorn	Dorn Fishing Facility	378 Bridge Ramp	3.8
Pavilion Cove	378 Bridge Ramp	Baker Creek Boat Ramp	1
		Total	5.4

ROUTE SIGNAGE AND AREA IDENTIFICATION:

—

Signage and maps are intended to provide a greater comfort level to the user, safety information, and brand identification for the project area. In addition to signage and mapping of the paddling routes, major coves and natural features on the Little River will be named and identified on the map. Presently the area has so few named landmarks that it doesn't have a sense of place and locations on the water are difficult to describe. Having named and identifiable locations is very important to the goal of establishing a more dynamic recreational culture on the Little River.

Signage should focus on put in and takeout areas as well as giving some navigational assistance in the larger sections of the river. In the upper sections of the routes, there is little need for signage other than at the takeouts. These sections are narrower and easy to follow. In the lower sections there is a greater opportunity for paddlers to make a wrong turn in the more open water and cove-laden shoreline. The Corps of Engineers will need to be consulted as to what the options and standards are for lakeside signage. The Corps can be a great assistance in showing how to best use the navigational and safety aspects of the signage.

With the permission of SC DOT, large informational maps could be placed under several key bridges using the "you are here" concept. This can be done in a manner that the maps cannot be seen by vehicular traffic on the roads. These check points will give an additional comfort level making the entire system more user-friendly.

Self-shuttling information will need to be developed showing directions to parking areas. Ease of accessing parking areas will be key to generating significant self-shuttling usage. In some organized paddling areas around the country, shuttling services are often operated either by private individuals or public agencies. Opportunities for shuttling services may be developed overtime as usage increases but may have early opportunities for existing canoe and kayak rental agents such as Hickory Knob or Baker Creek if a rental program is instituted in the future.

RECREATIONAL MOTOR BOATING
—

While the Blueway routes are primarily intended for paddlers, success in promoting the area will also increase motorboat usage. The upper sections of the system were not suited to motorboat traffic. Part of the draw for motor boating vacationing is having places to cruise to and a destination for a boat outing. Most recreational boating visitors unfamiliar with the area would be hesitant to go very far from their launch point at the various campgrounds without detailed destination information. Hickory Knob presently has the only water accessible food and beverage service in the project area. Including boating distances to the Hickory Knob Lodge from the other primary camping facilities could increase traffic to that location benefiting both Hickory Knob and the surrounding campgrounds. With a stated goal of increasing all campground usage, more recreational activity opportunities available for campers staying in other campgrounds would be more likely to extend their stay.

- Motorboat Routes (Hickory Knob Distances)

Sections	Put-In	Rest Area / Take-out	Length in Miles
To Baker Creek	Baker Creek Boat Ramp	Hickory Knob	8.25
To Hawes Creek	Hawes Creek Boat Ramp	Hickory Knob	6.3
To Leroy's Ferry	Leroy's Ferry Boat Ramp	Hickory Knob	5
To Mt. Carmel Mt.	Carmel Boat Ramp	Hickory Knob	8

II.
Hiking and Mountain Bike Trail Mapping

There already exists significant mileage of hiking and mountain biking trails in the project area. However there are no consolidated maps of these areas showing them as a system. In order to build multiday experiences, show the many places that a visitor can experience while basing out of one of the area campgrounds or lodging facilities is important.

Consolidating a GIS database of these assets and showing the interconnectivity will only enhance the usability and marketability of all the assets. It will also help in showing areas where mountain biking may be prohibited due to environmental sensitivity.

III.
Scenic Loop

While researching the river access of this project it was found that the series of roadways, primarily forest service roads, connecting these points was very scenic and incorporated many of the historical elements in the area suitable for vehicle or bicycle touring. Unlike a scenic highway, these loops supply visitors with activity options while keeping them in the project area.

Designating a route and supplying interpretive information as part of the overall recreation system adds another element that can be enjoyed by visitors of all abilities. Designating this route will allow campground visitors a morning or afternoon outing that may extend their stay. At minimal cost for signage this is another easily developable asset to include in the system.

The scenic loop proposed is a 48.5-mile loop traveling through Willington and Mt. Carmel and incorporates stops at the Indian Massacre site, Huguenot Worship site, and the Badwell Cemetery, home site and springhouse. Additional stops at the De La Howe Barn and interpretive trail, the De La Howe Tomb Site and other historic sites could easily be incorporated with the cooperation of the various owners of the sites.

IV.
Ongoing Recreational and Cultural Programming

The intent of programming is to use events at the existing facilities to build an outdoor recreation destination and build an outdoor recreation culture in the region. In looking at successful destinations throughout the region several common themes emerge. Small scale clinics and education on specific sports have a significant draw for increasing overnight accommodation rates on an ongoing basis. The competitive type events draw a larger number of users during a specific timeframe.

In looking at programs, we will focus on more than one target market. All the target markets would be equally beneficial to existing commercial entities such as restaurants and hotel operations. Our two main target audiences include the family oriented recreational users and the avid experienced outdoor sports enthusiasts.

Currently, most existing facilities lend themselves to a target market consisting of family oriented beginner to novice in recreational activities. These users are more likely to use rental boats, bikes, and guide & shuttle services. This group is more likely to use less challenging trails such as the Savannah Valley Rail Road Trail and the shorter sections of the river trail system. Attracting this group requires easy access to well mapped facilities and a well-planned itinerary for family/small group outings. This demographic is also available retail locations.

Experienced outdoor enthusiasts are more interested in the challenging aspects found throughout our project area. Challenging trails are already in place at Hickory Knob and Baker Creek State Parks. The area already hosts the Hickory Knob International Triathlon and the 2010 World Mountain Biking Summit was held at the FATS trail in southern McCormick County and eastern Edgefield County. Organized large group events and easy to use training trails and routes are attractive to this market.

An entertainment element has a key economic impact. Evening entertainment opportunities supplied by lodging assets or smaller commercial restaurant operations change the nature of the outing from a daytrip to overnight stays. It also draws campers and lodgers into the larger commercial community.

Kickoff Event

SUMMARY:

—

In order to build media attention to the project and draw initial attention to the area, a kick-off event is scheduled for August 14, 2010 at Baker Creek State Park. This will be a multi-scope event to feature paddling and mountain biking education and clinics. The kickoff will be followed up with periodic (possibly monthly in season) smaller outdoor events and tying into existing events such as the Hickory Knob Triathlon.

PURPOSE:

—

• Draw media attention to Northwestern McCormick

County and existing recreational infrastructure
- Increase outdoor recreation business and industry awareness of the area
- Establish an annual event based at Baker Creek State Park
- Test feasibility of ongoing monthly concerts in season for Baker Creek Pavilion Area.

EVENT ELEMENTS:

—

- Education about Little River Blueway Project and other McCormick County opportunities
- Paddling events and education.
- Mountain Bike events and education
- Afternoon/Evening concert

LOCATION:

—

Concert to be centered on Baker Creek Pavilion area with staging situated to allow viewing from both the Beach Area and Boats in Pavilion Cove. Paddling and mountain bike elements centered on courses are to be determined.

- Potential Partners and Sponsors:
- Palmetto Paddlers
- SORBA
- Augusta Canoe & Kayak Club
- AWOL – Augusta
- Chain Reaction – Augusta
- Confluence Watersports
- Half Moon Outfitters
- Various Media Sponsors

Periodic Paddling and Mountain Biking Events

While both paddling and mountain biking are individual activities, they are very social activities. There are many clubs and groups that regularly travel for organized multi-day outings. The project area is very suitable for these organized groups. The majority of participants in both these user demographics tend to use areas allowing a variety of skill levels and age ranges for these outings. A database of clubs should be developed to facilitate direct communications of opportunities and events. Regional clubs and commercial outfitters can and will coordinate many of these events if there is sufficient ease of access to the recreational infrastructure. Examples:

- Multi-skill level races/tours
- Clinics / Demo Days
- Moonlight Paddles

Monthly Music Series (In season)

In order to further promote multi-day usage of campground facilities and build a boating culture, periodic concert events could be staged at the Baker Creek Pavilion Cove serving both a land based audience from the campground and a boat based audience both from other campgrounds and the local population.

CONCERT SERIES BASED AT BAKER CREEK PAVILION

—

- Saturday afternoon/ evening shows to promote overnight camping
- Timed to coincided with paddling/ mountain biking events when possible
- Staging situated to be viewed from beach area and boats in the cove to promote a lake culture and a destination for locally based boaters
- Use popular local bands out of Greenville, Columbia, Augusta, and Athens to draw those markets.

Blueway Area Support Asset Catalog

Scenic Drive/Bike Route with Interpretive Guide:

1. Future Business Development Locations
- Willington on the Way District
- Mt. Carmel
- Hwy 378 and Hwy 28 Entrance Corridors

2. Land Based Trails
- Hickory Knob Hiking and Mountain Biking Trails
- Baker Creek Hiking and Biking Trails
- Forest Service Trails and Roads
- Corps of Engineers Trails and Roads
- Rails to Trails Program (Currently in Place)

3. Land Based Organized Recreation Assets
- Hickory Knob Golf Course- SC PRT
- Tara Golf Course - SLV
- Monticello Golf Course - SLV
- McCormick CC Golf Course – Privately Held
- Hickory Knob Skeet Range- SC PRT

4. Existing Camping Assets
- Baker Creek State Park -SC PRT
- Hickory Knob State Park -SC PRT
- Leroy's Ferry Campground – USACE
- Mt Carmel Campground – USACE
- Hawe Creek Campground – USACE
- Mt. Pleasant Campground – USACE

5. Scenic and Historical Assets
- Calhoun Mill Dam
- Little River Quarry
- De La Howe Tomb

- Indian Massacre Grave Site
- Huguenot Worship Site

6. Existing Lodging Assets
- Hickory Knob State Park -SC PRT
- Savannah Lakes Resort and Conference Center – Privately Held

7. Food and Beverage Assets
- Hickory Knob Lodge - SC PRT
- Monticello Grill -SLV
- Tara Clubhouse -SLV
- The Thai Café – Willington, Privately Held

8. Group Rental Facilities
- Mims Center - Willington
- Hickory Knob Lodge
- Hickory Knob Red Barn
- SLV Activity Center
- SLV Clubhouse
- Savannah Lakes Resort Conference Center

9. Motorboat Support Assets
- Village Store – Fuel and Groceries
- Savannah Lakes Marina –Fuel, Boat Rental and Supplies
- Hickory Knob – Fuel, Canoe/Kayak Rental
- Rays - Fuel and Groceries

10. Fishing Tournament Facility
- Dorn Fishing Facility – McCormick County

Wildlife Management Areas:

1. Other Assets

- Old Highway 378 Visitor Center Building (Presently Unused)
- Quail Woods De La Howe Youth Camp
- De La Howe State School Wilderness Program
- De La Howe Barn and Interpretive Trail
- Savannah Lakes Medical Center

2. Outside Significant Assets within 5 Miles
- Palmetto Anglers – Fishing Supplies/Guide Services
- McCormick Inn Bed and Breakfast – McCormick
- McCormick Arts Council
- McCormick Chamber Visitor Center
- Dorn Mill
- Gold Mine

River Access Points by Section

Little River Sections:

1. Calhoun Mill Steel Bridge (Proposed)
- Just south of Calhoun Mill Dam on 823 east of Mt Carmel
- Moderate open space in bridge ROW adjacent to F.S. road just east of bridge

2. Would need turn-around/ parking area and a steep bank access point:
- Mars Bridge Access (Proposed)
- Mars Bridge Road East of Mount Carmel
- Old roadbed abandoned on NW side of bridge giving good access to oxbow section. Several viable put in areas within oxbow area. The archeological significance of the area could prove problematic in developing any significant put-in parking area.

3. Morrah Bridge Backwaters (Proposed Improvements)
- On Morrah Bridge Rd east of Mt. Carmel
- Unofficial access area - would need improvements for heavy use

4. Little River Quarry Bridge (Existing)
- On Hwy 81 east of Willington, west of De La Howe State School
- Existing put-in area on western side of river south the bridge with parking

5. Long Cane Creek Boat Ramp (Existing)
- FS 33-227 From Huguenot Parkway
- Existing put-in with parking and picnic tables

6. Huguenot Worship Site (Existing with slight modification)
- Huguenot Parkway to FS 252-6
- Existing access road and parking

7. Buffalo Creek Boat Ramp (Existing)
- SCS-33-317 Barksdale Ferry Road
- Existing ramp and parking

8. Baker Creek State Park (Existing)
- Huguenot Parkway
- Existing Ramp, Parking, Camping Infrastructure

9. Highway 378 Boat Ramp (Existing)
- NE Of 378 Bridge

Long Cane Creek Sections:

10. Bradley Bridge Access (Proposed)

- Long Cane Road at the old covered bridge supports

11. Patterson Bridge Access (Proposed)
- Old Charleston Road

12. 28 Bridge Access (Existing)
- NE of Hwy 28 Bridge
- Existing ramp and Parking

Buffalo Creek Sections:

13. Badwell Cemetery Access (Proposed)
- Access off of Forest Service Rd. near Badwell Cemetery

Dorn Section:

14. Dorn Fishing Facility (Existing)
- Access off S33-124

15. Hawe Creek Campground Ramp (Existing)
- Access off
- Existing Ramp, Parking, Camping Infrastructure

River Access Analysis

Existing boat access ramps are in place to service the lower 7.3 miles of the Little River route and the lower 6.4 miles of the Long Cane route. While this area is presently usable, adequate river access upstream from these points is key to the making the Blueway a significant destination for paddlers long-term. The long-term project would consist of fourteen access points. Eight of these exist as operating boat access areas at the present time. Variety of access points allow flexibility to the users offering a range of river trail distances, time requirements and variety of river type experiences. Six new access areas are proposed.

These are the Calhoun Mill Steel Bridge Access, the Mars Bridge Access, the Badwell Cemetery Access, the Patterson Bridge Access, the Morrah Bridge Backwaters Access, and Bradley Bridge Access. Proposed access is only for paddling boats eliminating the need for ramps etc. necessary for trailer boat launch.

1. **Calhoun Mill Access:** The first proposed access would be the starting point on the upper section of the Little River. The Calhoun Mill Steel Bridge is a natural northern starting point for this project as it is immediately downstream of the historically significant Calhoun Mill Dam. The addition of this access point would add 9 miles of additional water trail upstream from the existing Little River Quarry Access on Hwy 81, which is presently the northern most official access area.

2. **Mars Bridge Access:** This would give a breakpoint on the long section on the upper section 2.5 miles downstream from the trailhead at Calhoun Mill. This site has an excellent location for a new access area with parking. When the new bridge was constructed on Mars Bridge Road, the road was rerouted to the new bridge leaving a road section to the old bridge abandoned within a major oxbow of the river. This is a significant archeological site and could be problematic.

3. **Badwell Cemetery Access:** A new access point on Buffalo Creek near the historically significant Badwell Cemetery, home site and springhouse. This also would open up a shorter 3.3-mile section on Buffalo Creek terminating at the Baker Creek State Park Boat Ramp. It would give access to the Badwell Cemetery as a point of interest. The cemetery is currently undergoing an extensive renovation by the Forest Service.

4. **Patterson Bridge Access:** This access would open up an additional 4.6 miles on Long Cane Creek north of the Hwy 28 Boat Ramp Access.

5. **Morrah Bridge Backwaters Access:** Improvements to the

existing unofficial access at Morrah Bridge Backwaters. This would give a breakpoint on the upper section 6.5 miles downstream from the trailhead at Calhoun Mill. This is a very interesting natural area.

6. **Bradley Bridge Access:** This access would be the trailhead for the Long Cane Creek Route adding 1.5 north of Patterson Bridge Access.

APPENDIX II

—

Selected Appendix

Andersen, K. (2009). Reset: How this crisis can restore our values and renew America, Random House LLC.

Berry, W. (1992). Natural Gifts, New Dimensions Foundation.

Berry, W. (1995). "Health is membership." Another turn of the crank 86: 90.

Berry, W. (1996). "Conserving communities." The case against the global economy: 407-417.

Berry, W. (2002). "The agrarian standard." Orion (Summer): 19-23.

Brown, B. (2012). Daring greatly: How the courage to be vulnerable transforms the way we live, love, parent, and lead, Penguin.

Brown, B. (2013). The gifts of imperfection: Let go of who you think you're supposed to be and embrace who you are, Hazelden Publishing.

Comte, A. and K. Thompson (1976). Auguste Comte: The foundation of sociology, Thomas Nelson & Sons, Limited.

Csikszentmihalyi, M. and M. Csikzentmihaly (1991). Flow:

The psychology of optimal experience, HarperPerennial New York.

Durkheim, E. (2014). The division of labor in society, Simon and Schuster.

Ereira, A. (1990). The heart of the world, Jonathan Cape.

Farrell, C. (2010). The new frugality: How to consume less, save more, and live better, Bloomsbury Publishing USA.

Flora, C., et al. (2005). "Community capitals: A tool for evaluating strategic interventions and projects." Avaliable from www.ag.iastate.edu/centers/rdev/projects/commcap/7-capitalshandout. pdf (accessed April 6).

Flora, J. and C. Flora (2004). "Building community in rural areas of the Andes." Social capital and poverty reduction in Latin America and the Caribbean: towards a new paradigm: 523-544.

Florida, R. (2010). Who's your city? How the creative economy is making where to live the most important decision of your life, Random House LLC.

Florida, R. L. (2002). The rise of the creative class: and how it's transforming work, leisure, community and everyday life, Basic books.

Jackson, K. T. (1985). Crabgrass frontier: The suburbanization of the United States, Oxford University Press.

Jacobs, J. (1961). The death and life of great American cities. New York, Vintage.

Jacobs, J. (1970). "The economy of cities." The economy of cities.

Marx, K. (2008). Das capital, DC Books.

Maslow, A. H. (1943). "A theory of human motivation." Psychological review 50(4): 370-396.

Mead, G. H. (2009). Mind, self, and society: From the standpoint of a social behaviorist, University of Chicago press.

Sheth, J. N., et al. (2011). "Mindful consumption: a customer-centric approach to sustainability." Journal of the Academy of Marketing Science 39(1): 21-39.

ABOUT THE AUTHORS
—

David Twiggs started in destination and resort management in 1990. Focusing on repositioning, brand management, product development, and completive advantage for private club and resort communities, he has been developing successful business models within real estate driven clubs and communities for the past 20 years.

As an AICP certified community development planner and an active executive for large-scale resort and retirement communities, David has a special interest in private community land use planning and business plan development. "To build an extraordinary place that has sustainable success, it must meet the needs of members, remain competitive in the marketplace, and maximize both traditional and non-traditional opportunities. This requires a multi-faceted approach incorporating, sustainability, profitability and quality of life. Redefining the function of the organization is vital if the long-term quality of life and property values are to be maintained and the investment of the owners is to reach its full potential."

David is active with the American Institute of Certified Planners, Club Managers Association of America, Community Association Institute, and the National Town Builders Association. Founding several regional branding non-profits and sitting on the boards of others, he takes an active role in shaping the community around him and urges clients to do the same. David, Ashley and their two daughters have recently relocated from

Augusta, Georgia to take up the challenge of reinventing Hot Springs Village in Arkansas, the largest gated community in the US.

—

Dr. Yang Luo-Branch Ph. D, native of China, came to the US to study when she was 23. She has extensive education and research experience in architecture, sociology, and urban planning. She taught at the College of Architecture of Texas Tech University for 4.5 years prior to joining the team of reinventing Hot Springs Village. Yang is the Director of Placemaking and Design with Hot Springs Village.

136

WHATS NEXT

—

Your purchase of this book is appreciated
and as a thank you, we would like to offer you
a FREE GIFT if you visit:

www.DavidTwiggs.com

Made in the USA
Charleston, SC
07 May 2016